While it is important that we bring new souls to Christ, it is essential that they understand the components of their praise. *Total Praise! An Orientation to Black Baptist Belief and Worship* helps them to do just that.

—Rev. Dr. Suzan Johnson Cook
pastor, Bronx Christian Fellowship Church and
president, Hampton University Ministers' Conference

Total Praise! An Orientation to Black Baptist Belief and Worship describes with clarity and insight how the Christian faith has found expression among Baptists. The essential nature of the Judeo-Christian heritage as practiced among Baptists is shared with accents on the practicality of faith for our contemporary age. This compendium of Baptist expressions of faith is an invaluable asset in understanding the contribution Baptists have made in translating faith into practice.

—Rev. Dr. William S. Epps
senior pastor, Second Baptist Church,
Los Angeles, California, and editor, *National Baptist Voice*

Total Praise! meets an important need in enabling lay and clergy readers to access important information and insights about the origins, development, and challenges facing African American Baptist churches across the country. The book walks the reader through the internal workings of church life within African American Baptist congregations. Through the use of study questions and suggested bibliographies for each section under review, this book offers a wealth of knowledge on one of the most important and enduring institutions within African American communities across the country.

—Rev. Dr. Marvin A. McMickle
pastor, Antioch Baptist Church, Cleveland, Ohio, and
author of *An Encyclopedia of African American Christian Heritage*

Dr. Lora-Ellen McKinney, having grown up in the parsonage of one of America's most effective pastors and administrators, the Reverend Dr. Samuel Berry McKinney, has observed in her own years of discernment the need for a re-presentation of some of the essentials of Baptist church and doctrinal teachings and faith practices. The format of *Total Praise!* makes it a very valuable teaching and orientation tool for New Members' classes. It is both informative and refreshing for persons with years of involvement in Baptist congregational life.

I commend Dr. McKinney for her contribution in authoring this book. I recommend *Total Praise!* to readers as a worthy addition to personal and church libraries.

—Rev. Dr. William J. Shaw
president, National Baptist Convention, USA, Inc.

Total Praise! is an exciting and important book. Lora-Ellen McKinney reminds us that one has to choose to be Baptist. The Baptist faith is not something that one is born into. At the center of our faith is a decision, a defining moment, that makes all of the difference in the world. McKinney attends to that initial decision by paying special attention to the history, rituals, beliefs, and practices that have shaped the experiences and unique contributions of African American Baptists. She demonstrates the power of questions as a way to grow into a living faith and deepen commitment. This is an important book because it provides comparative information with other faith traditions and offers an overview of our faith. The author provides useful information for church and denomination leaders, education programs, music and worship experiences, and social outreach. The title—*Total Praise!*—is well deserved.

—Rev. Dr. Archie Smith Jr.
the James and Clarice Foster Professor of
pastoral psychology and counseling at the Pacific School of
Religion and Graduate Theological Union, Berkeley, California

Total Praise! makes an important and unique contribution to ever-needed literature on worship in the African American tradition of Christian worship. Dr. McKinney stands in the rich tradition of Christian scholarship, alongside her father, Dr. Samuel Berry McKinney.

—Rev. Dr. J. Alfred Smith Sr.
professor of preaching and church ministries,
American Baptist Seminary of the West Berkeley, California,
and pastor, Allen Temple Baptist Church, Oakland, California

Dr. Lora-Ellen McKinney has supplied us with an invaluable manual of the basic beliefs and history of African American Baptist people. Dr. McKinney has given to Christendom a priceless description of the worship patterns of Baptists who are African American. The bibliographical references alone comprise a treasure trove for all who would understand a people, once slaves, who have achieved a cordial marriage of what is African and what is European.

—Rev. Dr. Gardner C. Taylor
pastor emeritus, Concord Baptist Church, Brooklyn, New York

total praise!

LORA-ELLEN McKINNEY

total praise!

An Orientation to Black Baptist Belief and Worship

JUDSON PRESS
VALLEY FORGE

Total Praise!
An Orientation to Black Baptist Belief and Worship
© 2003 by Judson Press, Valley Forge, PA 19482-0851
All rights reserved.

Judson Press has made every effort to trace the ownership of all quotes. In the event of a question arising from the use of a quote, we regret any error made and will be pleased to make the necessary correction in future printings and editions of this book.

Unless otherwise indicated, Bible quotations in this volume are from the New Revised Standard Version of the Bible, copyright © 1989 by the Division of Christian Education of the National Council of Churches of Christ in the United States of America. Used by permission. All rights reserved. Other quotes are from *The Holy Bible*, King James Version (KJV).

Library of Congress Cataloging-in-Publication Data
McKinney, Lora-Ellen.
    Total praise! : an orientation to Black Baptist belief and worship / Lora-Ellen McKinney.
      p. cm.
    Includes bibliographical references.
    ISBN 0-8170-1438-1 (pbk. : alk. paper)
    1. African American Baptists—Religion. 2. African American Baptists—Doctrines.
    3. Baptists—Religion. 4. Baptists—Doctrines.   I. Title.

BX6447.M35 2003

286'.173'08996073—dc21   2002067640

Printed in the U.S.A.

09 08 07 06 05 04

10 9 8 7 6 5 4 3 2

To my family, through blood and adoption,
here and gone, for their love of God and me

Contents

SECTION 1
Baptist Beliefs and Practices

SECTION 2
Dynamics of African American Religious Traditions

APPENDICES

Preface

Total Praise! An Orientation to Black Baptist Belief and Worship had to be written. In a time when increasing numbers of people are entering the faith and many are interested in learning about basic Baptist beliefs, we require easy-to-read, insightful tools that remind us just what it means to be black and Baptist in the United States. I am more than happy that the author, my elder daughter, felt led because of her life's experiences and faith convictions to make this contribution to ensure the presence of knowledgeable believers.

Lora-Ellen's family background played an important role in her growth and development as a Baptist believer. My mother's father (her paternal great-grandfather), Samuel Timothy Berry, was licensed to preach at the Sixteenth Street Baptist Church of Birmingham, Alabama, and was instrumental in the establishment and undergirding of several churches in that community.

Her paternal grandfather, Wade Hampton McKinney Jr., was the son of a Georgia sharecropper. He graduated from Morehouse College, received his religious training at Rochester Theological Seminary (where he wrote his thesis on the history of Negro

Baptists), and pastored two churches in his long career. My father served the Mount Olive Baptist Church in Flint, Michigan, for five years and offered his life on the altar of the historic Antioch Baptist Church of Cleveland, Ohio, for the next thirty-four and a half years.

I, Samuel Berry McKinney, was born in Flint, Michigan, reared and educated in Cleveland, Ohio, and, like my father, am also a proud graduate of Morehouse College and Colgate Rochester Divinity School. I assisted my father at Antioch Baptist for two years and, with my bride, was called to my first pastorate at the Olney Street Baptist Church, in Providence, Rhode Island, where our first child, Lora-Ellen, was born. After three years and three months in New England, I became the pastor of the Mount Zion Baptist Church in Seattle, Washington. Lora-Ellen attended public and private schools in Seattle, excelling in her studies. She has been an avid reader since she was very young and developed a social conscience early—Lora-Ellen grew up exposed to the civil rights struggle through discussions in our home and through observations of the challenges to her people that were occurring "down home."

My daughter, who has spent extensive amounts of time on the Asian, African, European, and South American continents, is a knowledgeable and curious international traveler. These experiences have contributed tremendously to her broad outlook, intellectual curiosity, acceptance of diversity, understanding of history, and informed worldview. She is also bicoastal in her domestic perspective. Born in New England and reared in the Pacific Northwest, she spent her freshman collegiate year at Spelman College in Atlanta and graduated from Vassar College in Poughkeepsie, New York. She received her master of science and doctor of clinical psychology degrees from the University of Washington in Seattle, and a master of public policy degree from the Kennedy School of Government at Harvard University. She is a brilliant woman whose educational achievements are most impressive and of which I am very proud.

Lora-Ellen's professional career has taken her to positions as a postgraduate trainee in Boston, a child psychologist in Harlem, and a pediatric psychology professor and director of programs for drug-exposed children in a San Francisco medical school. In Washington, D.C, she was a consultant on pediatric health care, the impact of substance abuse on children and families, environmental health, educational inequities, and leadership in nonprofit organizations. For her innovative work and volunteer spirit, she has been honored with a Kellogg Leadership Fellowship and a Salzburg Fellowship, through which she and other young leaders from around the world used the South African truth and reconciliation model to develop regionally appropriate recommendations for peace in the Balkans and the Middle East.

A natural question might arise, "Why would someone with all of this educational exposure, travel experience, and professional expertise be so concerned about the church, and in particular, the African American Baptist church?"

Let me suggest some answers. First, Lora-Ellen was reared to give back to her community, remembering that to whom much is given, much is required (see Luke 12:48). Second, she is an insightful woman who asks questions, seeks answers, and applies her intellectual gifts to making sense of the world. Finally, she has become an active member of the churches where she resides, and in all cases she approaches church membership with a supportive yet critical eye. (In fact, my heart goes out to those who have been her pastors, for I know from firsthand experience that she will seek truth until her curiosity is satisfied, her questions answered, and her spirit calmed—processes that can take some time.) Above all else, I believe that Lora-Ellen has used her talents to provide a resource for the African American Baptist church out of her love for Christ, her family, and the church, as well as the strong desire to see that the people of God order their steps in such a manner that all things are "done decently and in order" (1 Corinthians 14:40, KJV). Such ordered steps, steps that facilitate the true understanding of our faith, lead souls to Christ. In Lora-Ellen's case, they have recently led to her ordination as a deacon in the Metropolitan Baptist Church in the nation's capital.

I am honored to contribute this preface for *Total Praise!*, my firstborn daughter's most excellent publication, a book that I know will enrich the life of the Baptist church and its believers for decades to come.

—Samuel Berry McKinney, D.Min., D.H.L., D.D.
pastor emeritus, Mount Zion Baptist Church, Seattle, Washington,
and author, *Church Administration in the Black Perspective*

Foreword

Dr. Lora-Ellen McKinney has given a precious gift to the church and to the body of Christ. *Total Praise!* is a much-needed contribution to the Christian church because it provides a meaningful resource for those who are unsure and who have questions about their faith.

If there is a tragedy in the contemporary church, it is the number of persons who attend church but don't know why. Regrettably, our pews are filled with persons who have learned the "language" of faith but have not been challenged to plumb the depths of theological meaning that undergird the faith. Even more to the point, many of those who come to the church never use the Bible at any other time. Thus, we have a generation of churchgoers who don't know the difference between the Old Testament and the New. At the dawn of the twenty-first century, the traditional "church" is struggling for survival, due in large measure to the astounding number of persons who are unable to articulate their faith or give any reason for the ways in which they act or fail to act upon their religious beliefs.

In many ways our worship within the African American tradition has taken on elements of entertainment and even showmanship. Worship must be more than a Sunday morning spiritual "fix."

Authentic worship is more than simply following the order of worship and going through the motions. Praise is more than a "shout." It has to do with a lifestyle that has something to shout about because of one's relationship with Christ. McKinney leads us to an appreciation of our rich and resourceful tradition of worship and praise and to an appropriate commitment to authentic worship that honors God and blesses God's people. This work is critical in that it helps seekers and seasoned church members to understand what they believe and why.

Total Praise! is written in a manner that is comfortable for persons at all levels of understanding. While this work raises substantive doctrinal and theological issues, the reader is gently guided to a new appreciation of the faith through written language that is definitive and concise. The reader will be challenged to think, to question, and, ultimately, to make critical decisions about his or her faith.

Lora-Ellen McKinney is an academic who has clearly retained the "common touch." As a child of the parsonage, she is well equipped to guide us through these meaningful discussions not only because of her significant history with the church but because of the engaging quality of her faith that is evident in her walk.

Read this work and be blessed.

—H. Beecher Hicks Jr., M.B.A., D.Min.
senior pastor
Metropolitan Baptist Church, Washington, D.C.

Introduction

One of the most exciting things about the Baptist faith is that *we choose it.* We cannot be born Baptist. Instead, when we are mature enough to understand the importance of the act, we must make a conscious decision to give our lives to Christ and to build his kingdom on earth. *Total Praise! An Orientation to Black Baptist Belief and Worship* talks about this choice, the traditions and beliefs of the Baptist church, and the ways in which African Americans praise God.

The purpose of this book is to provide for new and established Baptists a quick and easy reference that details the basic beliefs and expressions of our faith and outlines the most important rituals of Baptist churches. The purpose is also to recognize the wonderful ways in which African Americans have praised God throughout our history in America. We flavor our praise with energetic and meaningful preaching, uplifting music, individual and collective prayer, personal expressions of joy, attention to the social issues that affect our community, and total involvement in church life.

Total Praise! provides a meaningful overview of our faith. It is meant to be useful for Sunday school and Christian education classes, in individual study, for developing church leaders, and as a training reference for students in the ministry. *Total Praise!* pays special attention to:

- *Christian beliefs,* namely in the attributes and teachings of Jesus Christ, the Son of God
- *Baptist beliefs,* including the priesthood of believers and the Great Commission
- *Baptist rites and rituals* such as believer's baptism and the Lord's Supper
- *Baptist commitments to essential freedoms,* among which are soul, Bible, church, and religious freedoms
- *Principles of church organization and management,* especially those related to the role of the pastor and church leaders and to typical patterns of organization
- *Guidelines for church participation,* including worship attendance, tithing, church etiquette, engagement in ministries, respecting the pastor and the pastor's spouse, prayer, and Bible study
- *African American traditions* of preaching, pastoral teaching, social action, and celebration of Christ through worship.

Each chapter of *Total Praise!* will encompass the following sections:

- **OVERVIEW:** a brief summary of the chapter topic.
- **THINKING THROUGH MY CHOICE:** questions and answers that explore chapter topics. The title for this section reminds us that we choose the Baptist faith. Answers will frequently include Bible verses to be used as opportunities for Bible study, reading beyond what is noted in the text. Because many of the Bible references come from the Gospels, readers may want to research parallel versions of the text cited, noting similarities and differences among Gospel records.
- **FYI:** materials that illustrate the chapter topic. Stories, sermons, and interesting ideas will be presented to enhance the reader's understanding of African American religious practices or the Baptist faith. African American religious songs or African American poems that relate to the chapter topic will also be included. Much African American poetry discusses religious faith and our perspective that Jesus has helped us through generations of toil and tribulation. Poetry will challenge the reader to think

about what the poet teaches us about faith.

• **THAT'S WHAT I'M TALKING ABOUT . . . :** several questions will be presented to stimulate discussions in Sunday school or other small-group environments.

• **PRAYERFUL CONSIDERATIONS:** written in the first person, these questions are posed to plumb the depth of the reader's commitment to his or her Baptist faith. The questions need not be discussed in a public forum but can be a starting point for personal conversations with God.

• **REFERENCES:** books and other resources that were used as research for each chapter.

To honor the history and traditions of the African American Baptist church, *Total Praise!* is divided into two sections. Section 1 focuses on Baptist beliefs and practices—those rituals, celebrations, and traditions that are particular to the faith and that distinguish it from other forms of religious belief. Understanding that African Americans praise God in unique ways, Section 2 discusses the dynamics of African American religious traditions with special attention to the richness of the African American Baptist form of praise.

As additional aids to readers, appendices provide information about Baptist and African American Baptist denominations, conventions, and affiliations; list references for readers who wish to read more about the topics discussed in the book or to do Internet research on those and related topics; and give more information about song titles used in the chapter headings. A glossary defines words and terms with which the reader might not be familiar or for which additional information would be useful. Words appearing throughout the book in **bold** (other than in section headings) will be found in the glossary.

Total Praise! cannot answer all of your questions about being Baptist, but it is a useful tool that engages you in thoughtful consideration of your faith choice, answers a range of questions about the beliefs and practices of the Baptist church, serves as a reminder of the meaning of those practices, and, most importantly, encourages you to join more fully with a like-minded community of believers who have chosen the Baptist faith as their way to live the Great Commission, to go into all the world and proclaim that Jesus Christ is Lord and that he is worthy of all of our praise.

In fact, the title of this book was selected to represent how African American Baptists seek to praise God. While we will surely fail on occasion, it is our goal to give God total praise. We have lived challenging lives in the United States and remain subject to the vagaries of racism and the ways it can affect all aspects of our lives. Nonetheless we laugh, we love, and we praise the God who has brought us through many difficult situations. We are fervent in our belief that Christ's goodness to us requires us to worship him with our whole hearts and beings.

As the song says, we should daily remind ourselves that God provides what we need for soul survival and spiritual sustenance. We are eager to live in a way that acknowledges our allegiance to Jesus Christ:

> *Lord, I will lift mine eyes to the hills*
> *Knowing my help is coming from you.*
> *Your peace you give me in time of the storm.*
> *You are the source of my strength;*
> *You are the strength of my life.*
> *I lift my hands in total praise to you.*[1]

---

1. "Total Praise," (Richard Smallwood) Copyright 1996 Zomba Songs Inc./T. Autumn Music. All rights controlled and administered by Zomba Songs Inc. (BMI)

Section 1

Baptist Beliefs and Practices

How Can You Recognize a Child of God?

The Exercise of Christian Faith

OVERVIEW

Baptists are Christians. Christianity is the world's largest religion, thought to have as many as two billion believers throughout the world. This chapter will briefly discuss the history of Christianity, its essential beliefs and practices, and some of its challenges. Readers will be asked to understand Christianity as a life commitment that requires its **adherents** to consistently strive to be faithful to their beliefs.

Jesus Christ, for whom Christianity is named, is believed by Christians to be the Son of God. Jesus' remarkable life and the history of Christianity as we know it are recounted in considerable detail in the New Testament of the Holy **Bible**. Although the history of Christ and Christianity requires more detailed explanation than it is possible to provide here, Christians agree on some sets of facts. Among these facts is this most important acknowledgment: that God gave his Son to the world so that the world could be saved from sin. To fulfill this promise, Jesus made the ultimate sacrifice of his life. Considered by the political forces of his day to be a dangerous revolutionary for his views that he was King and that allegiance was owed to him and not the Roman state, Jesus was condemned to death at thirty-three years of age. Nailed to a cross positioned between the crosses of two criminals and left to die as punishment for his crimes, Jesus understood the power of his suffering. As he was dying, Christ made several final statements, to which we now refer as the "seven last words of Christ." In the African American Church, Good Friday worship services tend to include these "words." Often each "word" is preached by a different preacher from the community. Good Friday services tend to be held between noon and 3 P.M., as 3 P.M. is thought to be the time when Christ died on the cross. The "seven last words of Christ" are found the most clearly in three of the four Gospels:

Word One: "Father, forgive them; for they do not know what they are doing" (Luke 23:34).

Word Two: "Truly I tell you, today you will be with me in Paradise" (Luke 23:43).

Word Three: (When Jesus saw his mother and the disciple whom he loved standing beside her, he said to his mother:) "Woman, here is your son." Then he said to the disciple, "Here is your mother" (John 19:26-27).

Word Four: "My God, my God, why have you forsaken me?" (Matthew 27:46).

Word Five: "I am thirsty" (John 19:28).

Word Six: "It is finished" (John 19:30).

Word Seven: "Father, into your hands I commend my spirit" (Luke 23:46).

After speaking these powerful words from the cross, Jesus died. On the morning of the third day following his **crucifixion**, Christ rose from the dead, a miraculous event that makes clear the divine nature of our Lord.

This chapter will address the following questions:

• What is Christianity?
• What are the central teachings and beliefs of Christianity?
• What is expected of Christians?
• What are some important events in the life of Jesus?
• What is a Christian?
• What is the Christian holy book?
• What is the most important Christian symbol?
• What holy days do Christians celebrate?

- What are the main branches of Christianity?
- What are the different views that Christians hold about Jesus?
- What do all Christians have in common, regardless of denominational traditions?
- How is Christianity similar to other religions?
- How does Christianity differ from other religions?
- What challenges has Christianity faced?
- How does one demonstrate Christian faith and belief?

THINKING THROUGH MY CHOICE

WHAT IS CHRISTIANITY?

Christianity is a relationship with Jesus Christ that begins when we ask for **salvation**. Asking Christ to forgive our sins and to let him guide our lives is the first step on a journey of Christian belief and practice.

WHAT ARE THE CENTRAL TEACHINGS
AND BELIEFS OF CHRISTIANITY?

Attributes of God: The one and only God who created our world is:
- *Omniscient:* God is all-powerful and all-knowing (Romans 11:33).
- *Omnipresent:* God is everywhere at all times (Deuteronomy 31:6-8).
- *Omnipotent:* God has complete and unlimited power (Genesis 1; Luke 1:37).
- *Love:* God is love. His love for us is represented in the gift to the world of his Son, Jesus Christ. In the Sermon on the Mount, Jesus made a clear statement about how much God loves us. "Look at the birds of the air; they neither sow nor reap nor gather into barns, and yet your heavenly Father feeds them. Are you not of more value than they?" (Matthew 6:26).
- *Supreme:* God reigns over all (1 Chronicles 29:11-12; Revelation 1:8).

Attributes of Jesus: Jesus is:
- *The Son of God:* All Christians believe that Jesus is God's Son, that he was born in human form to Mary and Joseph (Matthew 1:18), that he was recognized to have prophetic powers at a young

4

age (Luke 2:49), and that as a man he grew into awareness and acceptance of his divinity.

• *God:* This belief is focused on the belief that God is three persons in one, God the Father (Creator), God the son (Jesus), and God the Holy Spirit, the divine Spirit whom God sent in Christ's name. This belief about the nature of God is known as the **Trinity**. As God, Jesus shares all of the attributes listed in the section above.

• *Unique:* Christians believe that Jesus is the only divine spirit who was or ever will be both God and human (John 3:31).

• *A moral teacher:* Jesus admonishes us to love God and to love our neighbor. Through his life and lessons he provides a model for how his followers should live. (Reference the parables found in the Gospels, often identified as the words of Jesus by the use of red ink.)

• *Love:* So that the world could be saved from sin, Jesus died. As a divine Spirit, as God, he had the power to save himself. Yet, as the old song tells us, "He would not come down from the cross just to save himself. He decided to die just to save me."[1] (See John 8:42; 13:1-2.)

Primary Christian beliefs:

• *Everlasting life:* Those who truly believe in Jesus and live according to his teachings will live with Christ forever in heaven (John 6:47).

• *Heaven:* the location of reward for a life of Christian practice and belief (Genesis 2).

• *Hell:* the location of Christian punishment, typically considered a fiery and painful place that is the devil's home (Matthew 8:12; Romans 1:18-20; Jude 1:7).

• *Justification:* The belief that God forgives our sins (Psalm 65:3; Colossians 3:13; 1 John 1:8-9).

• *Regeneration:* The view that those who believe in Christ will be reborn in him (saved) (John 1:12-13; 14:6; 1 Peter 1:18-19).

• *Resurrection:* The belief that following his crucifixion and death, Christ rose (was resurrected) from the dead to sit at the right hand of God, his father. Jesus' resurrection was further proof of his divinity (Matthew 28:5-10; John 6:38-40).

• *The Second Coming:* Jesus will one day return to earth and will take all believers to heaven with him (Acts 1:10-11; 1 Thessalonians 4:16-17; 1 Peter 4:7-8).

WHAT IS EXPECTED OF CHRISTIANS?
- *Baptism:* **Baptism** is a sacred rite that represents the process of being reborn in Christ. Believers are baptized in or with water, a substance that symbolically washes away their sins. There are three forms of baptism: full **immersion**, aspersion (sprinkling of water), and affusion (pouring of water). Some Christians baptize infants, while others, including **Baptists**, mandate baptism of adults only.
- *Belief:* John 8:24 states that anyone who intentionally denies Jesus will die for his or her sins. These "words are also a sober reminder to Christians . . . that one's eternal destiny rests upon what one thinks of Christ."[2]
- *Bible study:* Christians are expected to increase their faith and their understanding of God through the study of God's Word as represented in the Bible (2 Timothy 2:15). A portion of this study should focus on **Christology**, the study of Jesus' life, works, and teachings. Bible study can be accomplished through individual study, in informal discussion groups, and in sessions taught by trained **theologians**. The Bible comes in many forms; there are now study Bibles that explain Bible history, clarify the meaning behind certain behaviors and practices, translate unfamiliar or foreign words, and make connections between common threads in Christ's teachings.
- *Church attendance:* The **church** is considered to be the Christian community; Christians are expected to join with the body of like believers in a service of **worship**, the purpose of which is to glorify Christ. Most Christians, including Baptists, celebrate Sunday as their holy day, because it represents the day of Christ's **resurrection** from the dead. However, the Seventh-Day Adventists and **Seventh Day Baptists** consider Saturday to be the **sabbath** (holy day).
- *Communion:* The service of **Communion**, also known as the **Lord's Supper**, commemorates Christ's sacrifice for us and allows his believers to engage his spirit in a service of adoration. During this service, bread and wine (or grape juice) are presented to the congregation as "the body and blood of Jesus Christ." Prayer and song are also important components of the service of the Lord's Supper, which Christ initiated (Matthew 26:26-29).

• *Commitment:* Faith requires us to believe what we cannot see but to seek God's face and favor through our Christian practice. Second Peter 1:5-8 says,

> For this very reason, you must make every effort to support your faith with goodness, and goodness with knowledge, and knowledge with self-control, and self-control with endurance, and endurance with godliness, and godliness with mutual affection, and mutual affection with love. For if these things are yours and are increasing among you, they keep you from being ineffective and unfruitful in the knowledge of our Lord Jesus Christ.

• *Confession of faith:* As Christians we must state affirmatively our belief in Jesus as the Lord and Savior of our lives (1 Timothy 6:12-16).
• *Great Commission:* Christ requires that Christians teach others about him, offer them a relationship with Christ, and baptize new converts in Christ's name (Mark 16:15).
• *Ministry:* Christians are required to **minister**, or serve others, as one way of serving Jesus. "Just as you did it to one of the least of these who are members of my family, you did it to me" (Matthew 25:40,45).
• *Prayer:* Prayer is communication with God for the purpose of thanksgiving, praise, confession, or special request, such as for the healing of an illness.
• *Submission or surrender to God:* Christians are expected to submit to the will of God. In our society, the idea of submission is often viewed as weakness. However, God requires our submission to him to make us stronger. When we submit to God's will, we allow our weaknesses to be replaced by his strength. God is all-knowing and all-powerful; if we trust in him and submit to his will for our lives, God will protect us and grant us his **grace** (James 4:6-8).
• *Worship:* Worship is defined as adoration. Christian adoration of Christ can happen in any setting on any day, not just in church services on Sunday morning. **Worship** can also have an **ecumenical** purpose, one that connects—through the unifying act of worship or prayer—the entire Christian Church.

WHAT ARE SOME IMPORTANT EVENTS IN THE LIFE OF JESUS? This brief summary recaps some important highlights in the history, development, and ministry of Jesus.

• *Birth:* The birth of the Son of God had been prophesied for many generations and was announced to growing numbers of persons who had awaited such a birth. Jesus was born in Bethlehem of Judea. His birth made royalty nervous, as they feared being displaced by this new king (Matthew 2:1-12).

• *The flight to Egypt:* Joseph, the earthly father of Jesus, was warned in a dream to flee to Egypt with his wife and child (Matthew 2:13-14).

• *Jesus went about his Father's business:* Jesus and his earthly family made a pilgrimage to Jerusalem to observe Passover. Once there, Jesus went off on his own; Mary and Joseph could not find him. After searching for three days, they located him in the temple, where he was listening to and intently questioning the teachings of learned men (Luke 2:41-49).

• *Jesus increased in wisdom and stature:* Upon his return with his family to Nazareth, Jesus learned his earthly father's trade of carpentry and continued his religious study so that he might be prepared for the work of his heavenly Father (Luke 2:51-52).

• *Baptism:* Jesus was baptized by his cousin, John.[3] As Jesus emerged from the water, John the Baptist saw the Spirit of God enter Jesus and knew then that Jesus was the Messiah (Matthew 3:13-15; Mark 1:9-11; Luke 3:21-22; John 1:32-34).

• *Wilderness wanderings:* When he had been baptized, Jesus heard God's voice acknowledge him as his Son (Matthew 3:14-17). Jesus knew that he must leave his home and family to begin God's work. To better understand the important undertaking that God had given him, he began a period of contemplation and communion with God. In the wilderness for forty days and nights, Jesus prayed and fasted, asking questions about God's will for his life (Luke 4:1).

• *Temptation by Satan:* While in the wilderness, Jesus climbed a high mountain. He had prayed throughout his vigil but had not heard from God. He began to doubt his mission and to lose courage. Jesus was also hungry and noticed at his feet small stones shaped like loaves of bread. As he looked at them, he heard a voice say, "If you are the Son of God, command the stone to become a loaf of bread" (Luke 4:3). Jesus knew this was the devil's voice and responded, "One does not live by bread alone" (Luke 4:4). As God's Son, he chose not to use his powers for physical comfort.

• *Gathering disciples:* His prayers for guidance answered, Jesus continued his journey. Along the banks of the Jordan River he saw his cousin John standing with his disciple, Andrew. John proclaimed, "Behold the Lamb of God!" Andrew ran to get his brother, Simon. Jesus saw in Simon the makings of an excellent disciple; he changed Simon's name to Peter, a symbol that Peter would establish the foundation of Christ's church (Matthew 16:18). Jesus, Peter, and Andrew began to travel and to collect other believers.

• *Miraculous works:* Jesus healed many people who were spiritually and physically ill. He also challenged old concepts of social status. Jesus spent a lot of his time with social outcasts and poor people, showing them God's love and mercy (John 9:24-26).

• *Last Supper:* The **Last Supper** was Christ's final Passover meal, eaten in the **Upper Room** with his disciples on the Thursday before his crucifixion (Christ died the following day, on Good Friday). At this meal Christ instituted the Last Supper (also called **Communion**) by breaking bread and drinking wine with his disciples (Luke 22:17-20), saying to them, "I have eagerly desired to eat this Passover with you before I suffer; for I tell you, I will not eat it [again] until it is fulfilled in the kingdom of God" (Luke 22:15-16). Jesus also let his disciples know that one of them would betray him (Judas had already begun preparations with palace chiefs about how he might betray Jesus for money, as described in Luke 22:3-6).

• *Trial:* Betrayed by Judas—one of his disciples—Jesus was arrested by soldiers and brought before the high priest, Caiaphas, and the Sanhedrin Council. Many people were bribed to tell lies against Jesus. Caiaphas asked Jesus to declare that he was God's Son and condemned him to death for blasphemy when Jesus would not honor Caesar but instead indicated that he was the Christ, God's Son and earth's King (Matthew 26:56-58).

• *Crucifixion:* Jesus was taken to Pilate, the Roman governor of Judea. Pilate believed Jesus to be innocent of the charge of blasphemy. Pilate declared that he could find no fault with Jesus and turned Jesus over to someone he trusted, a man named Herod. Herod, however, was more concerned with political power than truth. Embarrassed when Jesus refused to answer his insulting questions, he sent Jesus back to Pilate. It was Passover, a time when the governor was allowed to release a prisoner. Barabbas, a murderer, was also one of Pilate's charges. Pilate asked them whether he should release Jesus or Barabbas. When the crowd and soldiers asked for Barabbas's release, Jesus was condemned to death in spite of Pilate's attempts to change their minds (Matthew 27:16-20; Mark 15: 1-15). Jesus was forced to carry his cross up Calvary, and upon reaching the top of the hill, he was nailed to the cross. Though he was in extreme pain, Jesus spoke to the criminals near him who were also condemned to death by crucifixion. One asked for his forgiveness, and Christ offered him eternal salvation. Jesus asked God to forgive those who crucified him. After three hours on the cross, Jesus gave his spirit to God (Luke 23:46) and died (Mark 15:20-26,34-37).

• *Resurrection:* Jewish law did not allow a body to be left on a cross overnight. Joseph of Arimathea approached Pilate for permission to remove Christ's body. Once permission was given, the body of Jesus was washed, wrapped in fine linen, and placed by Joseph in his own tomb. Several women who loved and ministered to Jesus during his life wanted him to have a special burial. Collecting oils with which to anoint his body, Mary (Jesus' mother), Joanna, and Mary Magdalene went to the tomb (Luke 23:50-56). Jesus was not there, but the tomb was open. The women ran to the disciples to tell them that Jesus had risen, just as he had promised (Matthew 28:5-7). This was evidence of the **divinity** of Christ.

WHAT IS A CHRISTIAN?

A Christian is someone who believes in Christ and his teachings, who "[trusts] in the biblical Christ,"[4] and who believes that Christ died on the cross as a sacrifice for the sins of the world. The term

Christian originally described the **disciples** of Jesus at Antioch and was for a time a derogatory term defining Christians as part of a cult of believers (Acts 11:26).

WHAT IS THE CHRISTIAN HOLY BOOK?[5]

The Christian holy book is the **Bible** and is widely used in all forms of public worship and other rites.[6] The Christian Bible consists of the Old Testament, thirty-nine books originally written in Hebrew, and twenty-seven books of the New Testament, originally written in Greek between A.D. 50 and 150. The New Testament is the section of the Bible that describes the life, teachings, and good works of Jesus.

Roman Catholics favor a Bible that has an Old Testament that includes the Jewish Old Testament and seven other books called the **deuterocanonical** books (**Protestants** call these books the **Apocrypha**). Protestants use only the thirty-nine books of the Jewish Old Testament. The New Testament is the same for the Protestant and Catholic versions of the Christian Bible.

There are different views about how the Bible was written. Some Christians believe that the Bible represents the undiluted Word of God, while other believe the Bible to be a holy work inspired by God and interpreted by humans.

The Old Testament, a set of books not presented in chronological order, describes the religious life of ancient Israel. The New Testament is the second portion of the Bible and describes the covenant (relationship) that God has established with his people.

There now exist many different translations of the Bible, each of which is a new interpretation of the original language. There are also versions that attempt to frame biblical teachings within current cultural contexts. For example, the most recent version, Today's New International Version (TNIV), which will be available in 2005, reinterprets the Bible through use of gender-neutral language. In the 1970s, the Cotton Patch version of the Bible used common urban phrases to connect with racial minority groups. In all of its forms, the Bible is the most widely read and owned book in the world.

WHAT IS THE MOST IMPORTANT CHRISTIAN SYMBOL?

The most important Christian symbol is the cross. When Jesus was crucified, the cross became an essential focus of Christian faith, representing that he loved us enough to die for us. The cross, then, is a symbol of God's love for the world.

WHAT HOLY DAYS DO CHRISTIANS CELEBRATE?

• *Christmas:* Christmas, celebrated on December 25 of each year, is considered to be the birthday of Christ.[7]
• *Lent:* Lent is a forty-day period[8] of prayer, fasting, reflection, and submission to God's will that serves as preparation for Easter. Roman Catholics observe the entire Lenten period, while Protestants are more likely to celebrate specific days such as Ash Wednesday and all Holy Week events.

◊ Ash Wednesday: At the beginning of the season of Lent, we are asked to consider the meaning of life and death as a way of understanding Christ's life, sacrifice, death, and resurrection. Ashes, a sign of death and a symbol of new life in Christ, are placed on believers' foreheads in the shape of the cross.

◊ Holy Week: The holiest week in the Christian calendar, from Palm Sunday to Easter, commemorates the death and resurrection of Jesus.

◊ Palm Sunday: This day celebrates the triumphant return of Jesus into Jerusalem. Upon his arrival, followers lined the roadside, shouted aloud, and waved palms to greet him.

◊ Good Friday: On this day, Jesus was hung on the cross and crucified.

◊ Easter: Celebrated in the spring of each year, Easter is the day when Jesus was raised from the dead, demonstrating his divinity.

WHAT ARE THE MAIN BRANCHES OF CHRISTIANITY?

The three main branches of Christianity are the **Roman Catholic**, the **Eastern Orthodox**, and the **Protestant**. Baptists are members of the Protestant branch, Christians who strongly believe that the church should be independent of hierarchical structure and governmental influences.

WHAT ARE THE DIFFERENT VIEWS THAT CHRISTIANS HOLD ABOUT JESUS?

Christians hold a number of different views about Jesus. These views range from descriptions of Jesus as a human being with prophetic capabilities to Jesus as **divinity**. Most Christian groups, including Baptists, view Jesus as both human (temporarily) and divine (eternally).

WHAT DO ALL CHRISTIANS HAVE IN COMMON, REGARDLESS OF DENOMINATIONAL TRADITIONS?

While the different branches of Christianity do not agree on the characteristics of Jesus or what makes him unique, all Christians believe that Jesus Christ is God's Son, the world's most important teacher, and the best model for how to live a moral, meaningful, and compassionate life.

HOW IS CHRISTIANITY SIMILAR TO OTHER RELIGIONS?

Christians, Muslims, and Jews are the world's primary **monotheistic** religions. They all believe in the concept of one God.

HOW DOES CHRISTIANITY DIFFER FROM OTHER RELIGIONS?

Christianity differs from other faiths in its belief that Jesus Christ is the Savior of the world. The Christian faith is based primarily on New Testament teachings and regards the Old Testament as a historical document that anticipates the coming of Jesus Christ, the Messiah.

WHAT CHALLENGES HAS CHRISTIANITY FACED?

Systems of religious belief are likely to experience a wide range of internal and external challenges:

• *External challenges:* Christianity's external challenges have come through conflicts with other faiths over its central beliefs. Christianity has been attacked by other faiths, and in the Crusades and the Inquisition has been the instigator of war.

• *Internal challenges:* Internal challenges in Christianity have often occurred over differences in the understanding of central beliefs and practices of the church. Some examples include:

◊ The **Lord's Supper**: Christians have a variety of beliefs about the actual presence of Christ in the commemoration of the Lord's Supper. Roman Catholics believe that during Mass the bread and wine are changed, in substance, into Christ's body and blood (a belief called **transubstantiation**). Though it has no basis in Scripture, this belief first appeared in the ninth century A.D., was formalized by the Council of Trent (A.D. 1545–1563), and was reaffirmed at the Second Vatican Council (1962–1965).[9]

The Christian belief of **consubstantiation**, forwarded by Martin Luther, holds that the body and blood of Christ coexist with the bread and wine used in communion services. "Luther illustrated it by the analogy of the iron put into the fire whereby both fire and iron are united in the red-hot iron and yet each continues unchanged."[10]

Baptists do not believe in either **transubstantiation** or **consubstantiation**. Baptists believe that the **elements** used to represent Christ's body and blood in the celebration of the **Lord's Supper** are purely symbolic.

◊ Social issues: Other internal challenges have been related to concerns about whether or in what way the Christian church should respond to social issues. For example, some Christian churches are conflicted about their responsibility for addressing issues such as abortion, capital punishment, and community health challenges such as HIV/AIDS. On these issues Baptists are as divided as the rest of society. See Chapter 9 for more information on the role of African American churches in response to social issues.

◊ Social practices: Christians of different denominations have different beliefs about acceptable social practices. For example, some Christians believe that the drinking of any alcoholic beverage or gambling of any kind are sinful, while other Christians do not.

HOW DOES ONE DEMONSTRATE
CHRISTIAN FAITH AND BELIEF?

The exercise of Christian faith and belief requires:

• *Baptism:* An initiation into the Christian church and faith through participation in this sacred ritual.

• *Obedience:* Obedience to God's laws and living according to Christ's example.

• *Observance:* Observance of Christian holy days, sacred rituals such as the Lord's Supper, and other celebrations.

• *Prayer:* A steady diet of prayer allows us to commune with God and cleanses our spirits.

• *Worship:* Regular worship within the community of those who also believe in Jesus.

• *Tithing:* Payment of one-tenth of one's income to the church to support its **ministries**.

• *Service to others:* Participation in church organizations and missions that provide meaningful service to others.

FYI

Negro spirituals are an important part of the African American Christian tradition. These songs conveyed Bible stories, spoke of absolute faith in a just God, and hid from white slave masters political messages about planned escapes from slavery and the wish for freedom. In fact, during times of war or other social upheaval, "suspicions were more easily aroused and previously tolerated slave practices came under much closer scrutiny. . . . The most innocuous sounding sermon, the most solemn, traditional hymns, might conceivably contain double meanings that were obvious only to the black parishioners. When they spoke or sang of delivery from bondage and oppression, with Old Testament allusions to Moses and the Hebrew children, the hope clearly lay in this world—'And the God dat lived in Moses' time is jus' de same today.'"[11] As whites became more aware of the subversive messages present in Negro spirituals, slave masters required that a white person be present at all religious slave gatherings.

"He's Jus' de Same Today"[12]

When Moses an' his soldiers,
From Egypt's lan' did flee,
His enemies were in behin' him,
And in front of him de sea.
God raised de waters like a wall,
An' opened up de way
An de God dat lived in Moses' time
Is jus' de same today.

THAT'S WHAT I'M TALKING ABOUT . . .

- Why are you a Christian?
- What is most challenging for you about being a Christian?
- How do you deal with the challenges of being a Christian?
- How do you benefit from your worship of God?
- What does the Negro spiritual "He's Jus' de Same Today" teach about African American Christianity?

PRAYERFUL CONSIDERATIONS

- How does the practice of Christianity enhance my life?
- What are my expectations of my relationship with Jesus?
- What does Jesus expect of me?
- How do I know that Jesus loves me?

REFERENCES

- Encarta Online Encyclopedia. www.encarta.com; hereafter cited only by URL.
- Litwack, Leon F. *Been in the Storm So Long: The Aftermath of Slavery.* New York: Vintage, 1980.
- Ogden, Greg. *Discipleship Essentials: A Guide to Building Your Life in Christ.* Downers Grove, Ill.: InterVarsity Press, 1998.
- Tsoukalas, Steven. *Christian Faith 101: The Basics and Beyond.* Valley Forge, Pa.: Judson Press, 2000.

NOTES

1. Anonymous.

2. Steven Tsoukalas, *Christian Faith 101* (Valley Forge, Pa.: Judson Press, 2000), 19.

3. John is known as "the Baptist" for his practice of cleansing people of their sins by full immersion in the river.

4. Tsoukalas, xiv.

5. www.encarta.com (keyword: Bible).

6. The Bible is also the sacred book of Judaism, although in the religious tradition of Judaism only the Old Testament is used.

7. Although historic evidence has more recently indicated that this exact date may be somewhat inaccurate, Christians hold to this date as the time to recognize the special gift that God gave to the world.

8. The actual time between Ash Wednesday and Easter is forty-six days. However, Sundays, normally considered to be feast days rather than days of fasting, are not counted.

9. www.christiancourier.com (keyword: transubstantiation).

10. www.christiancourier.com (keyword: consubstantiation).

11. Leon F. Litwack, *Been in the Storm So Long: The Aftermath of Slavery* (New York: Vintage, 1980), 23.

12. Anonymous, Negro spiritual.

Becoming Baptist

Baptist Beliefs and Traditions Past and Present

OVERVIEW

Old and rich in history, the Baptist faith is an outgrowth of the Protestant Reformation that began in sixteenth-century Europe. The original Baptists were a fiercely independent group of Christian **adherents** who believed that they could have a direct and personal relationship with Jesus Christ and who rejected the union of church and state that was prevalent throughout Europe.

The Protestant Reformation was a revolutionary movement begun by a German priest and **theologian**, Martin Luther, in 1517. Luther challenged established religious practices of the **Roman Catholic Church**, the preeminent form of Christianity at that time. Specifically, Luther took issue with the Catholic belief that Christians are saved through their good works. Luther was convinced that Christians are saved by a conscious acceptance of Jesus Christ as their personal savior and by God's **grace**. Luther was also quite concerned that the Catholic church had too much influence over the European political system; he firmly believed that the Christian church should function separately from the state.[1] Finally, Luther believed that Christians did not require priests or other intermediaries to speak to God for them. Instead he believed that through a covenant relationship with Christ, they have direct and meaningful access to their Savior.

Protestant Reformers, later called simply **Protestants**, were revolutionary thinkers who wished to reform the traditional system of religious faith, belief, and practice. Protestants believed in:
• *Justification by faith:* The first step in a covenant relationship with Jesus required that believers make a public confession of faith.
• *The authority of the Scriptures:* The **Bible** is the Word of God.
• *The priesthood of all believers:* This implies direct access to God and responsibility as ministers. Every Christian is responsible for building Christ's kingdom.

Baptists, as one of many Protestant groups, share these beliefs but implement them in their own way. This chapter briefly discusses standard Baptist **dogma** and practices, setting the stage for the next chapters that will delineate specific beliefs, among which are:
• Soul freedom
• Authority of the Scriptures
• Church autonomy (separation of church and state)
• Believer's baptism (immersion)
• The Lord's Supper
• Spreading the Gospel throughout all nations.

In exploring Baptist beliefs and traditions, this chapter will address the following questions:
• Why are we called Baptists?
• What are the historical roots of the Baptist faith?
• What is the history of Baptists in the United States?
• What are the main components of Baptist theology?
• What are the main beliefs and **distinctives** of Baptists?
• How is the Baptist mission movement related to Baptist beliefs?
• How has Baptist theology affected American ideas of freedom?
• What is the Baptist view of the nature of God?
• Is there a **creed** or philosophy of religious practice that Baptists follow?
• What are the most important ordinances (religious practices) of Baptists?
• How does one become Baptist?
• What are the usual categories of admission to membership in black Baptist churches?

- How are infants and children incorporated into the life of a Baptist church?
- What are the responsibilities of Baptists to their church and faith community?

THINKING THROUGH MY CHOICE

WHY ARE WE CALLED BAPTISTS?

There is some indication that Baptists existed in the 1500s, though the name was not initially accepted because it was too similar to that of the **Anabaptists**, Christians who rebaptized persons who had previously been baptized as infants. Because of the extreme nature of some of their beliefs and practices, Anabaptists were held in low esteem by Catholics and some Protestant groups.[2]

It was not until the 1600s that English Baptists began to use the name *Baptist* to describe themselves.[3] **Baptists** are named for John the Baptist, the cousin of Jesus. John the Baptist was a prophet who foresaw the coming of the Messiah, believed Jesus to be the Messiah, and practiced adult **baptism** by full **immersion** (Matthew 3).

WHAT ARE THE HISTORICAL ROOTS OF THE BAPTIST FAITH?

The origins of Baptist theology, belief, and practice are connected to English Congregationalism, a late-sixteenth-century religious movement that rejected the parish structure of the Church of England. (A parish is the neighborhood surrounding a specific church building; all community members were required to belong to the parish and its church, and neighborhood children were automatically baptized into the faith.)

Protestants developed the "gathered church" model as an alternative to the parish structure. Membership in the gathered church was voluntary, based on evidence of spiritual conversion, and baptism was typically reserved for adult believers. Although their members were primarily English, the earliest Baptist churches (1609–1612) were located in Holland, a country with a reputation for religious tolerance. The first Baptist congregation, led by John Smyth, included thirty-six men and women. In 1612 Thomas Helwys returned to England from Holland and established the first English Baptist church.

All of the world's Baptists are part of a tradition that is most reliably traced to the seventeenth century (1600s). "This tradition has emphasized the lordship and atoning sacrifice of Jesus Christ, believer's baptism, the competency of all believers to be in direct relationship with God and to interpret Scripture, the influence of the Holy Spirit on individual lives and ministries, and the need for autonomous congregations free from government interference or hierarchical **polity**."[4]

WHAT IS THE HISTORY OF BAPTISTS IN THE UNITED STATES?
In England, Baptists were social outcasts, persons in need of a place to **worship**. They were strong believers in religious freedom as well as in the separation of church and state, and they were not practicing Anglicans (members of the Church of England).[5] Formerly a **minister** in and a member of the Church of England, Roger Williams was expelled from England because of his religious differences with the throne.

With other Pilgrims, Williams traveled to Massachusetts, a British colony, where he resumed his work as a minister. However, he was distressed by the influence of the church on civic affairs in the Massachusetts Bay Colony. In Massachusetts, Williams was threatened with death for his beliefs about church autonomy.

Williams escaped to uncolonized Rhode Island and in 1639 established the first Baptist church in America. This action made Rhode Island the first government in history that was founded on the belief in absolute religious freedom. Williams was the first American to be baptized by full immersion.[6] Another Baptist church was started around the same time in Newport, Rhode Island, by John Clark, a minister and physician.[7]

WHAT ARE THE MAIN COMPONENTS OF BAPTIST THEOLOGY?
While early Baptists did not share a single theological view, most believed that free worship requires soul competency (freedom), responsibility before God, and church autonomy (see other questions later in this chapter).

Baptists also exercised their religious freedom of belief and practice in other ways. Some Baptists based their **theology** on **Calvinism**, which believes in **predestination**, the concept that God has determined every action and outcome in the world and, by extension, those who benefit from God's **grace**. Other Baptists embraced **Arminianism**, the view that **free will** is the essential determining factor in **salvation**. General (Arminian)[8] and Particular (Calvinist) Baptists were the first two distinct groups of Baptists and Baptist thought. Calvinist Reformed theology was predominant by the eighteenth century, a time when Baptists became heavily involved in evangelism and overseas missionary work. Today Baptists are more typically Arminian in their theology, stressing free will, evangelism, and discipleship.[9]

WHAT ARE THE MAIN BELIEFS AND DISTINCTIVES OF BAPTISTS?

Baptists have a unique interpretation of the Protestant beliefs described in Chapter 1. Important Baptist beliefs might be listed as categories of freedom:

• *Soul freedom:* Baptists believe in the priesthood of all believers, the capacity of each believer to communicate directly with God as part of a sacred covenant, and the ability of each believer to practice faith without government interference.

• *Bible freedom:* Baptists believe in the authority of Scripture and in its centrality to our lives as individuals and within our community of believers. Baptists also strongly believe in our individual right to interpret Scripture as led by the Holy Spirit, not as dictated by church leadership.

• *Church freedom:* Baptists believe in church autonomy, the independence of every local church. Under the leadership of Jesus Christ, a Baptist church is free to determine its leadership, the ways in which the congregation worships, and forms of outreach and ministry.

• *Religious freedom:* Baptists believe that people should be free to practice their faith as they wish, without interference from informal bodies or state regulation of belief and practice (that is, they believe in separation of church and state). There are many different Baptist groups and a resulting number of differing beliefs, a fact that is not surprising if we think about the importance in Baptist faith of the concept of autonomy.

HOW IS THE BAPTIST MISSION MOVEMENT
RELATED TO BAPTIST BELIEFS?

The Baptist mission movement has an interesting history. During most of the seventeenth and eighteenth centuries, missionary work outside of the North American continent was unheard of. Adoniram Judson (1788–1850), the Baptist gentleman for whom Judson Press is named, was a well-known missionary. Born to a strict Congregationalist minister, Judson lost his faith during his college years. Reclaiming it after a prolonged spiritual struggle, he attended seminary and became interested in overseas mission work after reading a book on work in Burma (India). As there was no missionary society to support him, he gathered a group of like-minded persons from his seminary and created The American Board. He resigned from the Congregationalists and solicited the American Baptists for support, though they had no missionary society at that time.

William Carey, a British citizen who lived from 1761–1834, was a powerful voice among a small group of Baptists who publicly interpreted the **Great Commission** to be a requirement dictating the action and attention of modern-day Christians.[10] Carey believed that "as our blessed Lord has required us to pray that His kingdom may come, and His will be done on earth as it is in heaven, it becomes for us not only to express our desires of that event by his words, but to use every lawful method to spread the knowledge of His name."[11]

As is often the case, it is difficult to track the contributions of persons of color. In the missionary arena, well before Adoniram Judson traveled to Burma or William Carey did his important work, George Liele, the preacher who as a slave established one of the first black Baptist churches (see Chapter 5, page 55), conducted personal missions to the Caribbean and sent missionaries to West Africa. Following the founding of Silver Bluff between 1773 and 1775, Liele moved across the Savannah River into Savannah, Georgia, where he was one of the founders of the First African Baptist Church. Liele gained his independence from slavery and enjoyed great success as a minister in that community. As the Revolutionary War became a reality (1770–1785), the British told him (a deliberate untruth) that if he stayed in Georgia, he would be re-enslaved by the Americans fighting for independence. Fearing re-enslavement, he went with a British group to Jamaica and there organized the Hanover Street Baptist Church. From that church he sent out missionaries to other Caribbean Islands and to the African continent. (See References (Pugh, Alfred), p. 32.)

Lott Carey (1780–1828; no relation to William Carey) was a slave who became an evangelist. Converted to Christianity in 1807, he joined the First Baptist Church of Richmond, Virginia; learned to read; and was later licensed by First Baptist Church to preach. Carey bought his freedom from slavery in 1813. A New Jersey man named William Crane came to town and, taking an interest in the young blacks in Richmond, worked with Lott Carey to organize the Richmond African Missionary Society. In 1821 Carey made his first trip to Africa and traveled from Norfolk to Sierra Leone. In 1822, when the colony of Liberia was founded, Lott Carey established Monrovia's first church, Providence Baptist Church.[12] The Lott Carey Baptist Foreign Mission Convention continues to be an active missionary organization.[13]

In later years, African American churches had to work outside of established missionary societies to contribute to missions in the African Diaspora. For example, in the 1940s when members of the Antioch Baptist Church in Cleveland, Ohio,[14] decided to become involved in foreign missions, they had to work through the Christian Missionary Alliance and other independent agencies because at that time "colonial powers (then in control of Caribbean and African nations) did not want African Americans missionaries stirring up the African masses. The U. S. State Department agreed with this position and mainline Christian denominations, including the Northern Baptists [see Appendix 1, page 114] acquiesced."[15]

The missionary movement has grown considerably since the early years of the movement. Most Baptists embrace the idea of missionary work, have missionary societies in their local church-es, and jointly conduct missionary work under the auspices of Baptist conventions and associations.

HOW HAS BAPTIST THEOLOGY AFFECTED AMERICAN IDEAS OF FREEDOM?

• The Baptist faith developed as a radical alternative to state-sponsored religion and control. Baptists strongly believe in religious freedom, the freedom to worship God as one chooses.
• America now holds dear the ideal of freedom.
• Rhode Island was founded by Baptists as a place that respected religious liberty.
• When Thomas Jefferson wrote a religious freedom bill in Virginia in 1786, it was actively supported by John Leland, a local Baptist pastor. Leland, a state delegate for the proposed federal constitution, also pushed for the issue of religious liberty to be included in the Bill of Rights.
• The First Amendment of the Constitution contains evidence of the Baptist influence on political processes. It reads, "Congress shall make no law respecting an establishment of religion, or prohibiting the free exercise thereof...."[16]
• By 1883 all U.S. state constitutions "affirmed the principle of separation of church and state with full religious liberty."[17]

WHAT IS THE BAPTIST VIEW OF THE NATURE OF GOD?

Baptists believe in the **triune** God—God the Father, Son, and Holy Spirit (also known as the **Trinity** and God the Three-in-One). Baptists also believe in a God whose attributes include love (1 John 4:8), mercy (Psalm 136:1; 2 Corinthians 1:3), goodness (Psalm 52:1; 1 John 1:5), grace (Romans 11:6; Ephesians 2:8-9), an unchanging nature (James 1:17), foresight (Acts 2:23; Romans 8:29-30), holiness (Revelation 15:4), faithfulness (Deuteronomy 7:9), and judgment (Romans 9:12). The God that Baptists serve is supreme (2 Chronicles 20:6). Pages 4–5 in Chapter 1 list additional attributes of God.

IS THERE A CREED OR PHILOSOPHY OF RELIGIOUS PRACTICE THAT BAPTISTS FOLLOW?[18]

Although **evangelical** Christians, such as Baptists, tend to believe that the Bible is a sufficient guide in matters of belief and religious practice, many Baptist **denominations** have established **creeds**, confessions, and covenants. These documents are designed to unify believers and provide a structure for teaching beliefs.

• *Articles of faith:* Also known as The New Hampshire Confession, these articles state the main beliefs of Baptists regarding the nature of God, expectations of church members, and the power of the body of believers to build God's kingdom through individual, family, and joint efforts. The purpose of articles of faith is to clarify the Baptist faith, to inform and educate church members, to provide a basis for fellowship, and to deal with controversy within the church about specific beliefs and practices.[19] (See the Appendix 3 for a list of the Articles of Faith.)

• *Covenants:* The historic Baptist Covenant (see Appendix 4) serves as a statement of faith among the congregation of Baptist believers. The covenant is typically read monthly as an affirmation of faith that precedes the **Lord's Supper**. The covenant is often found in the front of hymnals. (Some Baptists use The New Hampshire Confession as a covenant statement or adapt its components for recitation in unison on Communion Sunday or for special ceremonies relevant to the faith.)

• *Creeds:* There are many historic creeds, of which the **Apostles'** Creed[20] is the most well known. Written around the fourth century, it is thought to have originally been used as a **catechism** for baptismal candidates. (See Appendix 5 for The Apostles' Creed.)

WHAT ARE THE MOST IMPORTANT ORDINANCES
(RELIGIOUS PRACTICES) OF BAPTISTS?

The two most important expressions of belief in Baptist churches are believer's baptism and the Lord's Supper.

• *Believer's Baptism:* It is impossible to be born into the Baptist faith. Each Baptist must choose Jesus for himself or herself; that is, Baptists adhere to believer's baptism. A person must make a confession of faith and engage in a voluntary ceremony of baptism by immersion. Baptism by immersion symbolizes a life changed by commitment to and relationship with Jesus. One enters the water a sinner; sins are symbolically washed away, Christ's salvation enters one's heart, and one is returned to the world, charged with living a Christ-like life. The act of baptism is a symbolic representation of our death, burial, and rebirth as new beings in Jesus Christ (Matthew 20:23; Mark 1:4; Acts 19:4; Romans 6:4).

• *The Lord's Supper:* The Lord's Supper is a symbolic reenactment of the last meal that Jesus had with his **disciples**. Frequently called **Communion** in the Baptist faith, it is a commemoration and celebration of the life, death, and resurrection of Jesus Christ (Luke 22:18-20). The term *Communion* reflects the practice of celebrating this service within a community of believers and is also the name for the **elements**, the bread and wine, which are essential parts of the ceremony. Baptists have two Communion practices:[21]

◊ Open Communion permits the participation in the Lord's Supper of any persons who believe themselves qualified to partake in the ceremony.[22] They may be Baptist, belong to other Christian groups, or may be members of no one particular congregation.

◊ Closed Communion restricts participation in the Lord's Supper to baptized believers who are members in good standing within their local congregations.

Most Baptist churches practice open Communion and celebrate the **Lord's Supper** on the first Sunday of each month.

HOW DOES ONE BECOME BAPTIST?

According to the *New Hiscox Guide for Baptist Churches*, membership in a Baptist church requires meeting four criteria:[23]

• *A regenerate heart:* The church is to be made up of members whose lives have been spiritually transformed (saved) and who believe that transformation to be the direct result of their relationship with Jesus Christ (Romans 6:22-23).

• *A confession of faith:* The Christian confession of faith in Jesus is the external expression of a profound internal change (Romans 10:10). The public confession of faith puts us in company with others who have been similarly converted, provides for us a community of like believers, and strengthens our capacity to work together to bring God's kingdom to earth.

• *A voluntary baptism:* Baptism is a physical manifestation of our public confession of faith. Baptists, unlike many other Protestant faiths, make the conscious choice to be baptized. Baptism is a cleansing ritual in which the sins of our former life are washed away and we are made pure to live for Christ and within the realm of his protection (Romans 6:4; Ephesians 4:5).

• *A Christian life:* Baptists must strive to live a Christian life according to the examples and teaching of Jesus Christ.

There are several categories of Baptist church membership and a variety of ways to join with the priesthood of believers within a Baptist church.[24] Though they may differ between churches, typical membership categories are:

◊ Full membership: This category is reserved for those who have made a public confession of faith and have been baptized. Full members participate in ministries of the church, contribute financial resources according to their personal means, cast a vote on important church issues, and engage in the fellowship opportunities provided by worship, Bible study, and other forms of Christian education.

◊ Nonresident parishioner: Nonresident parishioners are full members who live at a distance from the church and, as a result, are not able to regularly participate in church services and activities.

◊ Associate member: Associate, nonvoting church members hold multiple church affiliations. They may be college students, military personnel, or businesspersons on temporary assignment to a city. While they are interested in participating in a local church, they do not wish to relinquish their home church membership. Some Baptist churches also provide associate membership to persons baptized in another faith who attend and participate in the church but do not wish to change denominations.

◊ Watchcare fellowship: This is a special category of membership that allows churches to include persons "who are not yet ready or fully able to join the fellowship by reason of age, spiritual conviction, or other considerations."[25]

◊ Inactive member: These members were once active but now are chronically ill or are otherwise unable to participate in worship and ministries. Members without known addresses are often placed on the inactive list.

WHAT ARE THE USUAL CATEGORIES OF ADMISSION TO MEMBERSHIP IN BLACK BAPTIST CHURCHES?

Categories of admission to a black Baptist church typically are:

• *Baptism:* A candidate for church admission may join by acknowledging that they wish to be voluntarily baptized and by making a confession of faith.

• *Christian experience:* This category of membership is reserved for believers who have been baptized and who have confessed their faith.

• *Letter:* Those who move to a new city but were formerly active members of a church can request that a letter be sent to a specific church in their new location. Indicating that they were church members in good standing, this letter transfers their membership to the new church.

HOW ARE INFANTS AND CHILDREN INCORPORATED INTO THE LIFE OF A BAPTIST CHURCH?

Children are an essential part of the Baptist community' of faith. They represent fresh souls who will one day choose Christ for themselves. In conjunction with their biological families, the church family is responsible for providing them with religious support and education. By regular attendance at services and activities, children learn the components of the worship service, have the opportunity for service through age-appropriate ministries, and learn about the life of Christ and the beliefs of Baptists in Christian education classes. The primary ways in which children are incorporated into Baptist church life are:

• *Dedication:* Baptists do not baptize infants but want to provide for children evidence of God's love for them. Families typically bring their children before the congregation for an infant dedication ceremony (also called a blessing), in which the child's soul is prayed for, godparents are named, and parents and godparents are reminded of their responsibility for the child's religious and spiritual education.

• *Sunday school:* Sunday school is the primary form of Christian education for children and young teenagers. It provides a structure for learning about the life and work of Jesus Christ and for understanding Baptist beliefs and practices as preparation for making the choice to be baptized. (Many churches now offer Saturday school as one of many Christian education options for youth. Saturday school represents an adjustment to the changing needs of congregants.)

• *Believer's baptism at the age of reason:* Most Baptist churches support believer's baptism at the age of reason—the age when a child is old enough to understand the decision that he or she has made. The specific acceptable age varies among congregations, but the earliest age for baptism tends to be around age seven or eight. Most youth are baptized in their teen years.

• *Worship:* Children participate in worship through attendance with their families and by participating in children's activities such as the children's or youth choirs and usher boards. Some congregations provide a separate church service that is specially designed to meet the developmental needs of children and teenagers.

WHAT ARE THE RESPONSIBILITIES OF BAPTISTS TO THEIR CHURCH AND FAITH COMMUNITY?

Baptists are expected to join fully with their church community, learn the beliefs of the Baptist faith,[26] study the Bible, assist with ministries, contribute their whole hearts and spirits to worship, and maintain membership in good standing according to the guidelines set forth by their local church. See Chapter 4 for more information on Baptist requirements for full church participation and membership.

FYI

Many Baptists believe in praising God out loud. We tend to be exuberant in our praise because we see daily evidence of the presence of the Lord in our lives, are thankful for his blessings, and are delighted by opportunities to serve him. Based on Psalm 150:6, this contemporary song of praise outlines all of the reasons why our praise is essential.

Praise Him[27]
Let everything that hath breath praise Him,
Praise Him, Praise Him....
For giving me life and strength praise Him,

Praise Him, Praise Him….
For waking me up this morn praise Him,
Praise Him, Praise Him….
For the Lord has been good to me,
I can't hold my peace,
I must praise Him!

THAT'S WHAT I'M TALKING ABOUT . . .

- Through what form of membership did you join a Baptist church?
- What has been your experience of the major practices of the Baptist faith (believer's baptism and the Lord's Supper)? In what ways do they contribute to your walk with God?
- What risks have Baptists taken to praise God throughout the faith's history?
- Is the Baptist faith still revolutionary? In what ways?
- As a participant in the life of a Baptist church, what talents, skills, and resources do you make available to enhance the ministries that serve your congregation and community?
- What does the song "Praise Him" teach about African American Baptist belief and practice?

PRAYERFUL CONSIDERATIONS

- Why did I join a Baptist church? What made it seem like the right place for me to seek and serve God?
- Do I live up to the expectations of the Baptist faith in belief, practices, and service? If not, how have I fallen short? What must I do to enhance my membership and my faith?
- What am I willing to sacrifice for my belief in Jesus?

REFERENCES

- Freeman, Curtis W., James Wm. McClendon Jr., and C. Rosalee Velloso da Silva. *Baptist Roots: A Reader in the Theology of a Christian People.* Valley Forge, Pa.: Judson Press, 1999.
- Goodwin, Everett C. *The New Hiscox Guide for Baptist Churches.* Valley Forge, Pa: Judson Press, 1995.

- McBeth, Leon H. *The Baptist Heritage: Four Centuries of Baptist Witness.* Baptist Sunday School Board—Baptist Book Stores, 1987. Website of the American Baptist Churches: www.abc-usa.org.
- Pugh, Alfred Lane. *Pioneer Preachers in Paradise: The Legacies of George Liele, Prince Williams, and Thomas Paul in Jamaica, the Bahamas and Haiti.* St. Cloud, MN: North Star Press of St. Cloud, p.15.

NOTES

1. To clarify his protest with the Catholic Church, Luther nailed a list of concerns, called the Ninety-Five Theses, to the door of Castle Church in Wittenburg, Germany. Luther was particularly concerned about the sale of indulgences, a fine that was paid for forgiveness of sins and that was being used to finance the building of St. Peter's Basilica in Rome. www.encarta.com (keyword: Martin Luther).

2. A strict, radical Protestant **sect** that disagreed with Catholic and other Protestant practices, **Anabaptists** believed that the church comprised a body of saints, mandated a literal translation of the **Great Commission** to go into the world and preach the gospel, practiced shunning for people thought to have broken God's laws, and refused to pay taxes or serve in the armed forces.

3. www.encarta.com (keyword: Baptists).

4. www.abc-usa.org; polity refers to the governmental structure of a church.

5. Anglicans recognize the British monarch and God as heads of state. Henry VIII (1491–1547) established the Church of England when he sought permission to divorce his first wife and the Catholic Church would not allow it.

6. Williams did not remain Baptist but later returned to the Congregational faith.

7. www.encarta.com (keyword: Baptists).

8. Historically, General Baptists forbade singing as part of worship, believing it to be carnal and frivolous.

9. www.abc-usa.org.

10. While Judson and Carey actually worked together, Carey is the missionary who is credited with contributing to Baptists the idea that missionary work is an essential soul-saving tool, for those served and for the missionaries.

11. Curtis W. Freeman, James Wm. McClendon Jr., and C. Rosalee Velloso da Silva, *Baptist Roots: A Reader in the Theology of a Christian People* (Valley Forge, Pa.: Judson Press, 1999), 150.

12. Lott Carey was also involved in political uprisings in this country, after which he was suspended from his ministerial position. He died in 1828 in a munitions explosion. For more information, see www.google.com, keyword: Lott Carey missionary.

13. www.lottcarey.org. See also Chapter 5, page 59, for more information on Lott Carey.

14. Rev. Wade Hampton McKinney, the author's grandfather, pastored Antioch Baptist Church in Cleveland, Ohio, from July 1928 to December 31, 1962.

15. Conversation with Rev. Dr. Samuel Berry McKinney on February 10, 2003.

16. www.house.gov/Constitution.

17. www.abc-usa.org.

18. Documents described here can be found in Everett C. Goodwin, *The New Hiscox Guide for Baptist Churches* (Valley Forge, Pa.: Judson Press, 1995), 225–71, 320.

19. Leon H. McBeth, *The Baptist Heritage/Four Centuries of Baptist Witness* (1987), 68.

20. This anonymously authored document was not written by the apostles. It was written in Greek and later translated into Latin.

21. Norman H. Maring and Winthrop S. Hudson, *Baptist Manual of Polity and Practice, Revised* (Valley Forge, Pa.: Judson Press, 1991), 170.

22. The author's father and grandfather reminded worshipers that Communion is "not to be used as a pacifier for their children."

23. Goodwin, 31–38.

24. Ibid., 38–41.

25. Ibid., 40.

26. Most Baptist churches provide classes for new members that teach the basic beliefs of the faith.

27. Nolan Williams Jr. "Praise Him." New-J Publishing, 2000. Used with permission.

Guide Me, O Thou Great Jehovah

Baptist Church Organization and Management

OVERVIEW

The church of God is an institution that must serve the needs of its faith community, obey legal regulations and tax guidelines, and manage itself responsibly in a manner that honors God. The church is in fact a business—it is charged with carrying out God's work on earth.

As independent and autonomous agencies, Baptist churches have considerable freedom to determine organization and management processes. Because of Baptist ideas about religious freedom, there is no oversight group that dictates Baptist structure, organization, and leadership. Nonetheless, as a strong congregational community, Baptists do feel the need to meet with others who share the specific beliefs of their faith. To meet this need, most Baptist churches affiliate with conventions, fellowships, or associations (described fully in Appendix 1). These groups often recommend organizational structures, educational materials, and management strategies to guide the work of local churches.

Additionally, the *Hiscox Guide*, a historic document that has undergone recent revision, often serves as a manual for establishing, organizing, and managing Baptist churches. It provides a wide array of model documents that individual churches or conventions can adapt for their use.

34

Christ understood that the church has spiritual and **secular** responsibilities (Matthew 22:21). He also knew that the church is a structure that must be managed to serve God, often in an unreceptive environment. This chapter will focus on the typical organizational structure of Baptist churches.

This chapter addresses the following questions:
- What is the Baptist form of polity?
- Who runs a Baptist church?
- Who are the leaders of a Baptist church?
- What training do church leaders receive?
- How are church business matters communicated to members?
- How does the congregation participate in church business?
- What roles do Baptist conventions, associations, and fellowships serve in assisting churches with management?
- What other resources assist Baptist churches with management?
- How are Baptist worship services structured?
- How can individual **parishioners** contribute to the work of a Baptist church?

THINKING THROUGH MY CHOICE

WHAT IS THE BAPTIST FORM OF POLITY?

Simply defined, **polity** means church government. Baptist church government is congregational. The **church** represents a congregation of like believers gathered for **worship**. The **congregation** selects the pastor to serve at its pleasure, approves the selection of church leaders such as deacons, accepts new members into their faith community,[1] and is responsible for voting on issues of church policy and procedure.

WHO RUNS A BAPTIST CHURCH?

Christ is the head of Baptist churches. Led by a process of prayer and trial sermons and interviews, the congregation selects a senior minister as their leader and representative. The congregation gives authority to the minister to run the church with the support of lay leaders and church staff. The congregation has the power to hire and to remove the pastor from the pulpit and is also responsible for voting on issues that are essential to the life of the church. Baptist churches typically have detailed legally binding documents—bylaws and constitutions—that outline the responsibilities of all church leaders and the congregation. The following chart illustrates the levels of responsibility within the Baptist polity.

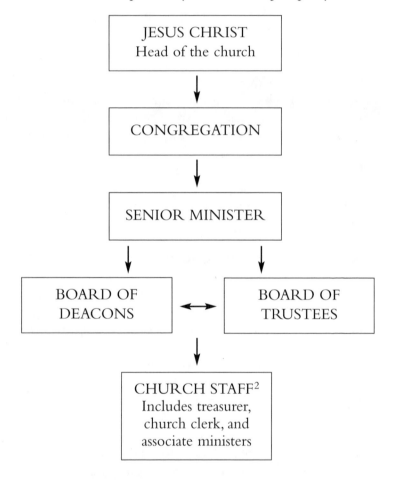

WHO ARE THE LEADERS OF A BAPTIST CHURCH?

Church leaders are expected to be Christians who behave ethically and understand that their role is to work for God's glory, not to achieve personal power.

Typical leaders in a Baptist church are:
- *The senior minister:*[3] The senior minister is charged with a variety of crucial and challenging tasks including:
  ◊ Management of the local Baptist church
  ◊ Leading the congregation according to God's will for them
  ◊ Inspiring, motivating, educating, encouraging, and counseling parishioners
  ◊ Planning the worship service and ensuring that the "proper implements of worship are employed." These implements include choral, congregational, and instrumental music; prayers; appropriate use of Scripture; sermons; and permission for personal expressions of joy such as hand clapping. "While there must be room for the Spirit to move, the pastor should have an order of worship which is both intelligent and ordered, yet flexible enough for the expression of the hearts of the people."[4]
  ◊ Attending to the intellectual and emotional needs of the congregation. Called by God to preach his Word and to bring souls to Christ, ministers are typically trained in Baptist theology in a seminary or Bible college.
- *Deacons,* who must be full church members in good standing, are pastoral assistants, help the senior minister carry out church policy and programs, and support the needs of church members. Deacons are recommended by the pastor for service and approved by the congregation. While deacons in the Baptist church are usually men, some churches have begun to ordain female deacons (Acts 6).
- *Deaconesses:* The Deaconess Board is made up of women, all full members in good standing (often the wives of deacons), who are special assistants to the senior minister. Nominated by the senior minister and elected by the congregation, deaconesses prepare the **elements** for **Communion**, visit the sick, and assist with funerals and meals for the families of the deceased. Many churches are moving away from the tradition of having deaconesses.
- *Trustees* are responsible for financial management and long-range church planning. In some Baptist churches, deacons and trustees are separate groups; in other churches deacons serve as trustees. As churches grow larger, many are instituting modern accounting

structures that change the traditional responsibilities of trustees.

• *Treasurer:* The treasurer is the church accountant and keeper of financial records.

• *Church clerk:* The church clerk records the minutes of church meetings, records voting and congregational processes, and manages church archives.

• *Council of Christian Education:* This group of lay leaders typically designs and runs the Sunday school, Bible study, and other Christian education classes, in line with Baptist beliefs and the pastor's vision for church growth and development as guided by the Holy Spirit.

• *Associate ministers:* Associate ministers are either ordained or are in training and serve the congregation at the pleasure of the senior minister. Associate ministers may serve as counselors for congregants, preach when asked, and are often given responsibility for the management of church ministries.

• *Other staff:* Churches may also have secretarial, sanitation, and other management staff as need requires.

WHAT TRAINING DO CHURCH LEADERS RECEIVE?
Church leaders receive different kinds of training according to their roles. Ministers, those who have been called by God to preach the gospel, must meet several requirements indicating their fitness to serve God's people in this capacity. Typical requirements are:

• *Licensure to preach:* Ministers recently called by God must be licensed to preach by congregational vote upon the recommendation of an ordained minister. While in training, licensed ministers are not given responsibility for church management.

• *Seminary training:* It is recommended that licensed ministers receive formal theological education in a seminary or a Bible college.

• *Ordination:* Ministers must be ordained, the act by which the church supports their call, training, and fitness for God's service through a public ceremony that celebrates partnership with God's people and dedication to Christian teachings.

Lay leaders (deacons, deaconesses, trustees, and ministry leaders) are trained for their specific roles by the senior minister, associate ministers, and other pastoral assistants. Church clerks and treasurers are expected to have excellent spiritual and training experiences that qualify them for their positions. Church leaders can also easily find literature and website resources to assist them in their training.[5]

HOW ARE CHURCH BUSINESS MATTERS COMMUNICATED TO MEMBERS?

Churches hold annual business meetings at which the senior minister, trustees, treasurer, and church clerk report on church finances. Full members are asked to attend the meeting, are usually given written reports, and may be asked to vote on plans for the next year's budget and programs. Churches also communicate business matters through announcements from the pulpit, in newsletters and bulletins, and as part of special "called meetings," meetings called by the senior minister and trustees to discuss issues of immediate importance to church functioning.

HOW DOES THE CONGREGATION PARTICIPATE IN CHURCH BUSINESS?

Full members of the congregation participate in formal church business by voting on matters of importance to church life. In alignment with local church bylaws and constitutions, the official board of the church (typically the senior minister, associate ministers, deacons, and trustees) makes recommendations to the congregation, which then votes on the presented issues. The church constitution will indicate whether or not a specific number of qualified members is required for a quorum.

Unless the church decides differently, votes on matters of legal significance are usually reserved for adult members of the congregation who are eighteen years of age or older. Other voting issues encompass all church members, including children under eighteen who have been baptized and have received the right hand of fellowship.

WHAT ROLES DO BAPTIST CONVENTIONS, ASSOCIATIONS, AND FELLOWSHIP SERVE IN ASSISTING CHURCHES WITH MANAGEMENT?

Although Baptist churches do not have an outside body that mandates church organization or recommends policy, local churches gather in a variety of conventions and associations that provide support. While conventions usually abide by the Baptist Covenant, they have different histories, differently interpret the Bible, and attract different members. Each provides resources for its members that include information on beliefs, perspectives on Baptist interpretation of or response to current events or issues, and lists of convention leadership and members. Some conventions and associations also provide online Bible study and links to other relevant websites. See Appendix 1 for more information on the history, founding dates, beliefs, website resources, and contact information for major Baptist conventions.

WHAT OTHER RESOURCES ASSIST BAPTIST CHURCHES WITH MANAGEMENT?

• *Church Administration in the Black Perspective* deals specifically with the management history and needs of black churches.

• The *Hiscox Guide for Baptist Churches* is an excellent resource. It has detailed historical information on church history and Baptist theology; outlines membership requirements; discusses leadership expectations; describes ordinances, ceremonies, and rituals; and provides copies of creeds, articles of faith, and covenants.

• *The Baptist Manual of Polity and Practice—Revised* also provides excellent materials on Baptist beliefs, church organization, structure, and recommended management.

• Religious bookstores and online booksellers also provide a variety of books on church management.

HOW ARE BAPTIST WORSHIP SERVICES STRUCTURED?

The order of worship[6] varies among Baptist churches but often follows a basic format. All formats tend to include devotion, a call to worship, prayer, Scripture reading, congregational singing, songs by the choir, an offering, a sermon, and a time when "the doors of the church are opened" to welcome new souls to Christ. Increasingly, Baptist services begin with time for praise. Praise singers lead the congregation in lively singing that celebrates the love of Jesus and asks worshipers to actively demonstrate their devotion to Christ.

Churches with a more formal style tend to use a church bulletin that provides the order of worship in considerable detail. Other churches believe that such structure interferes with the flow of the Holy Spirit. While all of the typical elements may exist in these services, the worship order is more variable and might not be announced.

HOW CAN INDIVIDUAL PARISHIONERS CONTRIBUTE TO THE WORK OF A BAPTIST CHURCH?

The church of God is people, and given its unique history this is especially true in the Baptist church. Baptists are admonished to be full members of their congregations and to maintain their membership in good standing. Chapter 4 discusses guidelines for full participation in the life of a Baptist church.

FYI

Servant leaders lead by serving others, a process that empowers all involved to reach their full potential. Servant leaders focus on meeting the needs of others and, through their actions, on building strong, functional communities. Although the concept of servant leadership was not designed to be applied to religious organizations, it has wonderful applications to the work of the church. This is evident in a story told in one of the many books available on servant leadership:

> Twelve ministers and theologians of all faiths and twelve psychiatrists of all faiths had convened for a two-day off-the-record seminar on the one-word theme of healing. The chairman, a psychiatrist, opened the seminar with this question: "We are all healers, whether we are ministers or doctors. Why are we all in this business? What is our motivation?" There followed only ten minutes of intense discussion and they all agreed, doctors and psychiatrists, Catholics, Jews and Protestants: "For our own healing," they said.[7]

41

THAT'S WHAT I'M TALKING ABOUT . . .

• Who are the lay leaders in your church? What are their roles and responsibilities? How is the congregation served by their work on your behalf?

• What are the differences and similarities between typical Baptist church organization and management and that in your local church?

• What is the order of worship in your church? How does the flow of the service contribute to your experience of worship?

• How is the goal of healing demonstrated in the organization and management of a Baptist church?

• In what ways is servant leadership evident in your church?

• What does the concept of servant leadership teach about African American Baptist belief and practice?

PRAYERFUL CONSIDERATIONS

• What is my role in my church?

• How can I support the leaders of my church?

• Am I a voting member of my congregation?

• What type of leadership can I contribute to the growth and development of my congregation and spiritual community?

• What are my needs for spiritual healing?

REFERENCES

• Asquith, Glenn H. *Church Officers at Work.* Valley Forge, Pa.: Judson Press, 1977.

• Goodwin, Everett C. *The New Hiscox Guide for Baptist Churches.* Valley Forge, Pa.: Judson Press, 1995.

• Greenleaf, Robert K. *Servant Leadership: A Journey into the Nature of Legitimate Power and Greatness.* Maryknoll, N.Y.: Paulist Press, 1977.

• Maring, Norman H., and Winthrop S. Hudson. *Baptist Manual of Polity and Practice—Revised.* Valley Forge, Pa.: Judson Press, 1991.

• Massey, Floyd Jr., and Samuel B. McKinney. *Church Administration in the Black Perspective.* Valley Forge, Pa.: Judson Press, 1976. Revised Edition published in 2003.

- McBeth, H. Leon. *The Baptist Heritage: Four Centuries of Baptist Witness.* Baptist Sunday School Board—Baptist Book Stores, 1987.
- McKinney, Lora-Ellen. *Christian Education in the African American Church.* Valley Forge, PA: Judson Press, 2003.

NOTES

1. When new Baptists join the church, the congregation is asked to accept them as members of the fellowship in full standing. African American Baptists typically celebrate new members by giving them "the right hand of fellowship" and singing songs such as "What a Fellowship" ("What a fellowship, what a joy divine, leaning on the everlasting arms").

2. Many churches now call these bodies "ministries" and design a board that consists of representatives of all church ministries.

3. Across **denominations**, the average church in the United States has approximately two hundred members and may not need more than one minister.

4. Floyd Massey Jr. and Samuel B. McKinney, *Church Administration in the Black Perspective* (Valley Forge, Pa.: Judson Press, 1976), 59.

5. Ibid.

6. The first known order of Baptist worship was designed in 1609. It included prayer, Bible verses (read and discussed), prophecy (sermon) for forty-five minutes, a second or third sermon as time permitted, a concluding prayer by the first speaker, and collection of the offering. Services were to be held from 8 A.M. to noon and from 2 to 5 or 6 P.M. See Leon H. McBeth, *The Baptist Heritage: Four Centuries of Baptist Witness* (Baptist Sunday School Board—Baptist Book Stores, 1987), 91.

7. Robert K. Greenleaf, *Servant Leadership: A Journey into the Nature of Legitimate Power and Greatness* (Maryknoll, N.Y.: Paulist, 1977), 36.

4

What Must I Do to Be Saved?

Guidelines for Church Participation

OVERVIEW

When we join the church, we ask Jesus to forgive our sins. We make a promise to him that we will live pure and holy lives. Because this is a difficult challenge, we work to maintain prayerful spirits and seek the support of others who share our beliefs in and commitments to Christ. As part of our commitment to him, we are asked to be energetically involved in the life of his church.

The goal of all forms of Baptist church participation is to provide opportunities for believers to serve God (Hebrews 13:16), to support and contribute to the community of Christian believers, to provide needed community services, and to bring new souls to Christ. This chapter addresses the expectations that must be met by Baptists to be church members in good standing. Among them are:

• Spreading the gospel throughout all nations
• Tithing
• Engaging in personal ministry
• Participating in Christian education on a regular basis
• Responsible stewardship
• Meeting informal expectations (church etiquette, pastoral support, respect and acknowledgment of the First Family).

This chapter addresses the following questions about church membership and participation:

- What is required for me to be considered a member in good standing in a Baptist church?
- How do I obey the requirements of the **Great Commission** within my church?
- Does the church have rules that I must follow?
- What happens if I do not fulfill my Christian obligations within my church community?

THINKING THROUGH MY CHOICE

WHAT IS REQUIRED FOR ME TO BE CONSIDERED
A MEMBER IN GOOD STANDING IN A BAPTIST CHURCH?
Baptist churches spell out a number of specific expectations for members. While it is true that no one monitors the activities of individual members, it is expected that each faithful Baptist will assure that he or she keeps the commitment made to Jesus when he or she confessed faith, was baptized, and joined the fellowship of believers. These expectations are:

- *Spreading the gospel throughout all nations:* Most Baptists are expected to bring new souls to Christ. African American Baptists often engage in evangelism, providing witness to others of the love of Christ and the **salvation** that he offers to those who are willing to follow him.
- *Tithing:* The word *tithe* is derived from an Old English word that translates as "one-tenth." Biblical tithing is a special kind of offering to God. It requires that we provide one-tenth of our income to the church to support its work and its ministries. In Malachi 3:10 (KJV) we read, "Bring ye all the tithes into the storehouse, that there may be meat in mine house, and prove me now herewith, saith the Lord of Hosts, if I will not open you the windows of heaven, and pour you out a blessing, that there shall not be room enough to receive it." Tithing is a huge commitment, but God deserves no less than this from us. Tithing is an exercise in obedience to God and a way to return to him a small portion of the riches with which he has blessed our lives (see Ezekiel 44:30).
- *Engaging in personal **ministry**:* Hebrews 13:16 teaches, "Do not neglect to do good and to share what you have, for such

sacrifices are pleasing to God." Serving the Lord requires serving his people. Church ministries are designed to provide congregants and surrounding communities with needed services and are also wonderful opportunities to spread God's Word. There are many forms of **ministry** in which congregants can become involved. Ushers, the gatekeepers of the church, serve by maintaining order in **worship** services. Choirs serve by sending spirits high with their songs of praise. Urban ministries address issues that affect the community and require a special commitment to serving "the least, the last, and the lost." Ministry participation allows congregants to keep their commitment to God and receive his favor for their dedication to service. "When you step forward, God magnifies his provision."[1]

• *Participating in Christian education:* Christian education classes provide church members with an opportunity to learn more about God's Word. Baptists are expected to enhance their relationship with Christ through a commitment to understanding his Word. Most Baptist churches hold Sunday school classes for all ages and offer Bible classes at least once a week. They may also offer Bible seminars on special topics, such as women of the Bible and the importance of prophecy, and workshops to help members improve their stewardship, such as scriptural principles for money management, rearing Christian children, and engaging in regular family prayer.

• *Practicing responsible stewardship:* Stewardship is the entire process by which we obey our obligations to Christ by managing our money, health, time, talents, and other resources in a responsible manner. Tithing is one form of responsible stewardship. Managing our time so that we balance our commitments to God, family, self, and work is another stewardship responsibility.

HOW DO I OBEY THE REQUIREMENTS OF THE GREAT COMMISSION WITHIN MY CHURCH?

Each Baptist church will have a variety of ministries in which you can be involved. It is important to identify your spiritual gifts and to use them to contribute meaningfully to the life of the church. Witnessing to others can help them take the first steps toward Christ; living a Christian life serves as a model for others to follow.

DOES THE CHURCH HAVE RULES THAT I MUST FOLLOW?
While there is no rulebook for Baptists, there are definite expectations about how **parishioners** should behave in church. These unwritten rules tend to fall into the following categories:

• *Honoring Christian symbols:* The cross, the Bible, the **Communion** table, and the baptismal pool represent Christ and his sacrifice to us. They should not be written in or on, leaned on, played with, or used in any manner that is contrary to their designated sacred purpose.

• *Maintaining a spirit of worship:* When we are in the church building, voices should be kept at a conversational level. In the sanctuary, parishioners should be silent and respectful during times of prayer and contemplation. Brief comments to pew neighbors must be conducted in a low voice. Ushers will direct the flow of traffic in and out of the sanctuary at the appropriate times. Congregants are expected to participate in the joyful moments of the worship service, joining in with singing and responding to the sermon as the Spirit moves them.

• *Respecting church property:* The church building is God's house and must be treated with a special measure of respect. Only ministers and invited guests are allowed to be in or to speak from the pulpit. Personal items must never be placed on the Communion table, and food, drinks, and chewing gum must be kept out of the sanctuary.[2]

• *Dressing to honor God:* While many African Americans dress up for church, it is important that we dress in a manner appropriate for worship. Clothing we might see in a nightclub is unlikely to be suitable for church. Very short skirts, low-cut tops, and overly sheer items should be carefully considered. In most African American churches jeans and casual clothing are not considered church attire, but this viewpoint varies from **congregation** to congregation.

• *Using appropriate language:* Street language does not belong in the church. In fact, Christians should challenge themselves to consistently use language that honors God, rather than switching language forms when they enter the church building. It is also important for church members to refrain from sowing seeds of dissention; they must remember that God is love and prayerfully guard against speaking negatively about other members of their Christian community.

• *Respecting the pastorate:* The senior minister of the church and all ministerial staff have received special calls from God to be responsible for a congregation and to serve them as God's undershepherds. The senior minister should receive respect for the special relationship that he or she has with God and is to be addressed with a title (Pastor, Reverend, Minister, or Doctor as appropriate). In the African American church, the pastor's family also has special status, resulting from their relationship to the head pastor and in recognition of the support that they provide for him. The pastor's wife[3] tends to be referred to as the first lady; she and her children are often provided with designated seats on a pew near the front of the church. Other ministers are also to be accorded respect.

• *Training our children:* One of the most important goals of the church is to "train children in the right way, and when old, they will not stray" (Proverbs 22:6). If parents and other adult parishioners model appropriate church behavior for their children, those young people will know how they are expected to behave in church.

WHAT HAPPENS IF I DO NOT FULFILL MY CHRISTIAN OBLIGATIONS WITHIN MY CHURCH COMMUNITY?

As a general rule, Baptists do not excommunicate those who do not fulfill their obligations to Christ or meet church expectations. John 8:3-8 tells the story of a community that wished to stone to death a woman observed in an act of adultery. When they asked Jesus if this punishment was fair, he replied that only those free from sin could participate in the stoning. Because we have all sinned, we must guard against being judgmental about the behavior of others. When people are engaged in sin, they require our support more than ever. African Americans are known to say, "The church is a hospital for sinners, not a hotel for saints." Nonetheless there are times when church members may be asked to account for their behavior by church leaders. Church leaders, including pastors, who abuse their authority may be asked to step down from their positions. The *Hiscox Guide* also provides a process for exclusion, which is dismissing an individual from church membership, responsibilities, and privileges by a vote of the congregation. *Hiscox* notes that "an act of exclusion should always leave open the possibility of restoration."[4]

FYI

"He Washed the Feet of Judas"[5]
Christ washed the feet of Judas!
The dark and evil passions of his soul,
His secret plot, and sordidness complete,
His hate, his purposing, Christ knew the whole,
And still in love he stooped and washed his feet.

THAT'S WHAT I'M TALKING ABOUT . . .
- Why does God require us to tithe our resources to the church?
- Why is it easier to share our talents and time than our money?
- What is the importance of witnessing to others about our faith?
- In what ministries do you participate? Why do you engage in those ministries, and what is the nature of your participation?
- What does the poem "He Washed the Feet of Judas" teach about African American religious belief, practice, and participation in ministry?

PRAYERFUL CONSIDERATIONS
- What are my skills and talents? How do I make them available to the church?
- What talents am I fearful of contributing to God through the church? How might I work past those fears?

REFERENCES
- Freeman, Curtis W., James Wm. McClendon Jr., and C. Rosalee Velloso da Silva. *Baptist Roots: A Reader in the Theology of a Christian People.* Valley Forge, Pa.: Judson Press, 1999.

- Goodwin, Everett C. *The New Hiscox Guide for Baptist Churches.* Valley Forge, Pa.: Judson Press, 1995.
- McBeth, H. Leon. *The Baptist Heritage: Four Centuries of Baptist Witness.* Baptist Sunday School Board—Baptist Book Stores, 1987.

NOTES

1. Brenda Girton-Mitchell, chair of the board of trustees, Metropolitan Baptist Church, Washington, D.C., February 13, 2002.
2. Responsible treatment of church property is another form of stewardship.
3. The majority of pastors are still men. However, whether one's pastor is male or female, appropriate respect should be accorded to the pastor's spouse and family.
4. Everett C. Goodwin, *The New Hiscox Guide for Baptist Churches* (Valley Forge, Pa.: Judson Press, 1995), 44.
5. George Marion McClennan, "He Washed the Feet of Judas," in *The Book of American Negro Poetry* (New York: Harcourt Brace Jovanovich, 1969), 97.

Section 2

Dynamics of African American Religious Traditions

5

Ain't Gwine Lay My 'Ligion Down

African American Baptist History and Traditions from Slavery to the Present

OVERVIEW

The history of the African American church and the religious worldview of African Americans are undeniably tied to our African past and heritage. Melville Herskovits once stated that slaves brought with them from West Africa a considerable amount of "invisible cargo," represented in the African traditions that today are part of our services of religious worship. Most Africans were not Christians when they were brought as slaves to America in 1619.[1] Others, however, might have found in Christianity familiar views taught as early as the second century when the Christian mission spread to North Africa, "one of the gospel's securest homes," and further south in Africa, to Nubia (see Acts 8:27).[2] As a result, though Africans arrived in America with specific cultural and religious beliefs and experiences, some of their religious practices may have been Christian or included Christian practices.

Dr. Henry H. Mitchell has conducted seminal research that indicates the many similarities between the doctrines of African traditional religion and Christian beliefs. These shared doctrines include the view of God as **omnipotent, omniscient, omnipresent, provident,** and just. "No slave master taught us that

God is just. We knew that very well before we came here, and there are hundreds of [African] proverbs to document this. The only new things to slaves were Jesus and Hell. The Bible had a new way of saying the rest of our basic worldview."[3] Among the Baptist practices that were similar to traditional African religious rituals was **baptism** by **immersion**, a practice that resembled a water rite of the river cults of West Africa.

African American religion is an interesting mix of historical African worldviews and our uniquely American slave-time conversion to, continuance of, or experience of Christianity, a faith whose foundation in one God resembled the traditional faith slaves brought with them from Africa. Some historians and religious scholars refer to the African worldview as the "black sacred cosmos," a set of beliefs that the universe is sacred, that engages believers in special religious rituals, and that respects certain sacred objects.[4] Cultural historians consider **religion** to be a social phenomenon, a system of faith and belief organized by people who wish to understand, worship, and reap the benefits of a relationship with a power greater than themselves. As is the case with people of all races and ethnicities, Africans were strongly influenced by their many histories and cultures.[5]

With a view of the world that held people and objects as universally holy and valuable, Africans (those brought to America and African Americans born into slavery in this country) had a peculiar experience when their slave masters introduced Christianity to them. Although they were enslaved, despised, mistreated, and devalued by whites, and although they were forced to sit in the balcony or stand outside the door of the church, Africans learned about the God of love. They could easily have decided to reject the religion of their slave masters, but they did not. Instead, our ancestors found in the Christian God someone to love and comfort them in the midst of their painful and degrading environment.

The Christian God ultimately revealed in Jesus of Nazareth dominated the black sacred cosmos. While the structure of beliefs for Black Christians were the same orthodox beliefs as that of white Christians, there were also different degrees of emphasis and valences given to certain particular theological views. For example, the Old Testament notion of God as an avenging, conquering, liberating [hero and champion] remains a formidable anchor of the faith in most Black churches.[6]

Jesus was thought to be a Savior not just of our souls—our ancestors believed that he would also provide divine rescue from earthly slavery and pain in addition to the reward of heaven for true believers.

As part of this tradition of black Christians, African American Baptists began the first black churches in America that were not extensions of larger white religious denominations.[7] "Following slavery and a long period of involuntary servitude, many African Americans chose to become Baptist because the faith valued freedom; choosing to be Baptist allowed us to be in charge of our own churches and religious destinies. As an old prayer says, African American Baptists believe that 'we are free to pick and choose our own praying ground.'"[8]

This chapter addresses the history, organization, culture, and challenges of the African American Baptist praying ground by posing the following questions:

- What is the history of African American Baptist churches?
- Do African American Baptists believe and worship differently from other Baptists?
- Historically, why did so many African Americans choose to be Baptist?
- Do African American Baptists have a unique interpretation of the Bible?
- What are typical forms of religious expression among African American Baptists?
- How are African American Baptist churches typically organized?
- Does the African American Baptist Church have **bishops**?
- What is the role of conventions in African American Baptist churches?
- What current challenges face African American Baptist churches?

THINKING THROUGH MY CHOICE

WHAT IS THE HISTORY OF AFRICAN AMERICAN
BAPTIST CHURCHES?

African American Baptists have the same Baptist beliefs and traditions of religious practice as the Europeans who started the faith
in the 1600s and those who later brought it to North America.
Once in America, black Baptist traditions of religious freedom
occurred alongside those of black Methodists and were similarly
timed to the American Declaration of Independence, which
pushed to free the American colonies from British political rule.

A man named Quassey was the first known black Baptist, reg-
istered in 1743 as one of fifty-one members of the Baptist **church**
in Newton, Rhode Island. There is controversy among historians
about which of two churches was the first African American
Baptist church. African Baptist or "Bluestone" Church was founded in 1758 in Mecklenberg, Virginia. While historical records
indicate that George Liele, a slave, established the Silver Bluff
Church on the Savannah River in South Carolina between 1773
and 1775, the church cornerstone lists 1750 as its founding date.

As churches were founded, they began to gather in convention
structures. "Fugitive slaves and free blacks in the North [formed]
abolitionist missionary associations and societies, the leaders of
which then organized the first regional black conventions. Many of
the participants of these associations were for a long time simulta-
neously involved in white Baptist organizations."[9]

African American Baptist churches lost some independence after Nat
Turner's insurrection.[10] "That movement sent hot hate back and wide
consternation all over the Southland. Generally, what independence
Negro churches had enjoyed was taken away. A revised black code was
enacted ... silencing ... colored preachers. A [white] church ... [and] association . . .would take a Negro church as a branch; and thus the independence of the Negro church was further postponed."[11] Today there are
"eight identifiable black Baptist communions in the United States."[12] The
largest are the National Baptist Convention USA, Inc. (NBC-USA), the
National Baptist Convention of America (NBCA), and the Progressive
National Baptist Convention (PNBC). The Lott Carey Baptist Foreign

Mission remains a powerful body serving black Baptists. (See Appendix 1 for more information on African American Baptist conventions.)

DO AFRICAN AMERICAN BAPTISTS BELIEVE AND WORSHIP DIFFERENTLY FROM OTHER BAPTISTS?

Baptists from all ethnic groups have the same basic beliefs and theology, although **worship** practices frequently vary as a result of cultural differences and perspectives, which fall into the following categories:

• *Theology:* African Americans of all religions bring components of their African heritage into their worship services. The forms of music that we sing in our praise of God, as well as the physicality of our praise (hand clapping, holy dancing, and lifting holy hands), are tied to our African roots. (See Chapter 8 for a discussion of the influence of historically African traditions on African American Christian music and praise.)

• *Revolutionary perspective:* The African American Christian perspective is also tied to the way our population grew in slavery. After the second generation of slaves was brought to America, more people were born into slavery in America than were brought from Africa. At the time of the Revolutionary War, one-fourth of the American population was black and enslaved. With such large numbers of slaves, accompanied by the tendency of whites to view religion as having a calming influence on the enslaved population, the revolutionary quality of slave religious practices (for example, songs that told slaves to follow the North Star to freedom) went unnoticed for a time, allowing more than three hundred slave rebellions to form. Most of them were led by black preachers.

• *Christian practice:* African American Christians may interpret religious traditions and practices in accordance with their experiences. For example, **Communion** traditions maybe uniquely interpreted. Miles Jerome Jones states that "to be *at the table* . . . is to realize that for some persons to come to the table means at first to overcome the hindrances imposed by hardship and denial."[13] As was previously mentioned, African American Christians also tend to maintain an Old Testament view of God as an avenging and protective Spirit who understands the struggles of the downtrodden and will bring them out of bondage, much as he did for the children of Israel.

HISTORICALLY, WHY DID SO MANY
AFRICAN AMERICANS CHOOSE TO BE BAPTIST?

Today the majority of religious African Americans identify themselves as Baptist, a statistic with a fascinating history. African Americans and the early white Baptists shared a history of being despised.

> The reason why the Baptist faith appealed so strongly to the Negroes is not far to seek. From the onset they had more in common with the white Baptists than with any other denomination. As the white Baptists were looked upon as an outgrowth of the Anabaptists, they were held in contempt by many. There were not many men of standing in this [white] church at first. Therefore, this church drew its members for the most part from the poorer class of people. As these did not own but few, if any, slaves, it was easy for them to oppose the institution of slavery.[14]

In choosing the Baptist faith, African Americans were also provided the freedom of the autonomous church. "Its local democracy enabled the Negro preachers to participate in the affairs of the church much earlier than any other denomination, and allowed people to worship God in their own way. The African heritage was given free play."[15]

DO AFRICAN AMERICAN BAPTISTS
HAVE A UNIQUE INTERPRETATION OF THE BIBLE?

Hermeneutics is the technical term for biblical interpretation. The African American hermeneutic has focused on several facets of interpretation:

• *New Testament teachings:* Although we believe in an Old Testament God who will lead us out of our social and spiritual wilderness, African American Christians focus on the life and teachings of Christ as found in the New Testament. The life of Christ is described in the Gospels of Matthew, Mark, Luke, and John. The remaining New Testament Scripture focuses on the **divinity** of Christ.

• *Liberation language:* Considered essential to how African Americans interpret the Bible, liberation language relates the ways that God and his Son work to set us free from spiritual and physical bondage. "From the story of Moses in the Hebrew Bible to Jesus' ministry to the poor and oppressed in the New Testament, African Americans have embraced the Word of God and made it their own."[16] African Americans have also strongly supported the idea that religious values should be interpreted within the context of personal experience. One result of this belief is the knowledge that God looks like us. Jesus was noted to have hair like lamb's wool (Revelation 1:14) and is known to be from a geographical region of brown-skinned people. On this issue, A.M.E. **bishop** Henry McNeil Turner once stated,

> We have as much right biblically and otherwise to believe that God is a Negro, as you . . . white people have to believe that God is a fine looking, symmetrical and ornamented white man. . . . Every race of people since time began who have attempted to describe God by their words, or by paintings, or by carvings, or by any other form or figure, have conveyed the idea that the God who made them and shaped their destinies was symbolized in themselves, and why should not the Negro believe that he resembles God as much as other people?[17]

Affirming that God is black is a component of liberation language, just as the ability to view and adore a painting of a black Jesus is a liberating experience for people of African descent. The bondage of slavery clearly shaped the African American attraction to a God who greatly loves, saves, sacrifices for, resembles, and frees his people, especially when the view has Scriptural support.

• *Development of African American theology:* A number of African American scholars have dedicated their careers to looking at Scripture through a lens colored by their cultural experience. This has resulted in a number of articles and books on African American biblical interpretation, some of which can be found in the Reference sections for each chapter as well as in the recommended resources (Appendix 2). Development of an African American theology has led to courses on African American theology in respected schools of religion and materials to assist ministers in "applying black biblical scholarship to the lives of the people in their congregations."[18]

WHAT ARE TYPICAL FORMS OF RELIGIOUS EXPRESSION AMONG AFRICAN AMERICAN BAPTISTS?

We are expected to go into the world, spreading God's Word, through methods including the following:

• *Living the Great Commission*

◊ Missionary work: Missionary work is very important to us. The African American mission movement was begun when Lott Carey established an African mission in Sierra Leone, West Africa, in 1821. The Lott Carey Baptist Foreign Mission Convention was formed in 1897 after a split with the National Baptist Convention over creating a separate black publishing house (see Appendix 1). Not wanting to lose access to resources of the American Baptist Publication Society or to lose votes as required by a merger, the Lott Carey group dedicated itself to foreign missions. Although the Lott Carey Baptist Foreign Mission Convention remains active in its foreign mission work, most of the larger black Baptist conventions now have well-funded missionary societies.

◊ Ministry to others: Designed as strategies for advancing economic and spiritual survival while living the **Great Commission**, church ministries feed the hungry, clothe the naked, and provide many important services that meet the needs of communities inside and outside the church (see Chapter 4 for more information on church **ministry**).

• *Evangelism:* Simply defined, evangelism is the spreading of Christianity for the purpose of converting souls for Christ. Missionary work is one form of evangelism. Other forms, more often seen in local communities, are:

◊ Revivals: Revivals are usually held in the spring in the weeks surrounding Easter, a time of spiritual rebirth. Revivals are week-long preaching missions designed to renew our spirits and assist us in reviving our commitment to Jesus Christ. Revivals were historically held in tents located in open fields, which allowed persons from surrounding towns to create a temporary **congregation** in which God could be praised. While "old-time" revivals can still be found, most are now held in churches. Revivals tend to be preached by visiting ministers or by full-time evangelists, traveling preachers without churches whose entire ministry is devoted to bringing souls to Christ.

◊ Lecture series: Many churches also hold lecture series, the focus of which includes pastoral teaching about a particular passage of Scripture, discussions about African American theology, or the application of Scripture to issues of social importance.

◊ Witnessing: Christians frequently tell other people about their conversion experiences. Through this process, Christians serve as witnesses to Christ's goodness to them. By explaining our experiences, we hope to bring new converts to Jesus.

• *Physical and emotive experiences in worship:* African Americans are often expressive worshipers, involving our whole bodies in our praise of God. There are several historical reasons for the physicality of our praise. In Africa, all religious and secular celebrations were accompanied by exuberant singing and dancing. Rhythm, mainly through the use of drums, was an African form of nonverbal language that allowed us to communicate with one another over long distances. We brought those traditions with us when we came to America as slaves. More recent reasons for our emotional responses in church are that our lives are frequently very hard. Church is for us a true sanctuary, a safe haven in which we are free to demonstrate our emotions (pain, disappointment, and happiness) in the presence of the family of like believers. Additionally, as African American Baptist churches increasingly gained from white Baptists the true autonomy of worship that is central to our beliefs, church became a place where we could celebrate outside the eyes and judgment of those who often mistreated us. In church we gave each other respect that was denied us in the world outside of church. Being called Mother, Sister, Brother, and Mister are still experiences worthy of celebration—that we can celebrate our humanity in a world that still denies it is evidence that God loves us. The most common forms of spiritual expressiveness among African American Baptists are:

◊ Getting happy: Also known as shouting, getting happy is a form of joyful dancing that may include arm waving, crying, calling upon God, proclaiming God's goodness, or falling onto the floor in religious ecstasy.[19]

◊ Hand clapping: Hand clapping often accompanies singing, acknowledges agreement with speakers, or thanks God for his goodness to us.

◊ Lifting holy hands: Believers often raise both hands toward heaven as a sign of respect for and adoration of Christ.

◊ Prayer: Prayer is the most common way that we use words to communicate with God. African Americans recognize our ancestry in our prayers by calling on the God of our ancestors.

◊ Speaking in tongues: Technically known as *glossolalia*, speaking in tongues is typically found in **Pentecostal** churches and in some Baptist congregations as well. It is thought to be a sign of religious perfection that represents an infilling of the Holy Spirit.[20]

◊ Standing to honor God: When moved by Scripture, sermons, or singing, African American worshipers may stand to honor God as a sign that they are moved by God's Word.

• *Self-help:* While self-help may sound like an odd category of African American religious expression, it is an essential part of our history and current behavior. The African American church has a tradition of self-help that is tied to our recognition that

> the Black Church is the most economically independent institutional sector in the black community. . . . The origins of the black self-help tradition were found in the attempts of slaves to help each other survive the traumas and terrors of the plantation system in any way they could. . . . Mutual aid or beneficial societies and churches were among the first social institutions created by black people.[21]

Modern churches are increasingly involved in community economic development. They have credit unions and banks, build affordable housing, and work with civic and political organizations to make certain that important stores and services are owned by racial minority group members and are located in or near communities of color. (Also see Chapter 9 for a discussion about the role of the church in addressing social issues.)

• *Dress:* Increasingly, African American Christians have found ways to bring African forms of dress into their religious traditions. For example, many churches are incorporating traditional African fabrics such as kente cloth into their worship services in the following ways:

◊ In ministerial or choir robes and stoles

◊ For special cultural events where the entire congregation celebrates by wearing African garb

◊ By making a personal decision to wear African dress to church on a regular basis.

• *Décor:* African American churches proudly display evidence of African heritage through:

◊ Use of African fabrics as lining for offering baskets or banners

◊ Displays of African art throughout the sanctuary and church building.

HOW ARE AFRICAN AMERICAN BAPTIST CHURCHES TYPICALLY ORGANIZED?

African American Baptist churches follow the same organizational structure as most Baptist churches. See Chapter 3 for information about the typical organization and management of Baptist churches.

DOES THE AFRICAN AMERICAN CHURCH HAVE BISHOPS?

The Baptist faith is not one that includes individual **bishops** and a collective **bishopric** as a higher category of pastoral responsibility. Because the Baptist faith does not have an oversight organizational structure outside of the structure imposed by each local church, it does not *typically* have **bishops**. Bishops tend to work within larger church organizations such as those provided by the Episcopal, AME, and Presbyterian denominations and the Catholic Church (the **Pope**, for example, is the head bishop of the Roman Catholic Church). These church organizational bodies provide qualifications for bishops, assign them to service, and train them for that service by positioning them in specific congregations and moving them up the hierarchy of the denomination. The Full Gospel movement within the Baptist denomination has created an informal **bishopric** that has some well-known church leaders. While individual Baptist bishops have done good work and are well-respected, the issue of the Baptist bishopric goes against Baptist history and **tenets.** As such, it is quite controversial within the **denomination.**

WHAT IS THE ROLE OF CONVENTIONS
IN AFRICAN AMERICAN BAPTIST CHURCHES?

Held each year, Baptist conventions provide for African American Baptists a place to meet and discuss the work of their individual churches and to collectively plan for activities and programs that advance Christ's teachings.

Historically, conventions provided a way for a group of local Baptists to provide support programs for newly emancipated slaves. When the Civil War ended in 1865, local Southern churches organized into an association to consolidate their resources. The first state convention was organized in North Carolina in 1866. By 1870 there were Baptist conventions in every Southern state, and a reported five hundred thousand African American Baptists were represented by them.[22]

African American conventions are also strongly tied to the missionary movement. Leroy Fitts notes,

> The evolution of an African mission was a strong motivating factor in the development of associations and conventions among black Baptists. The primary objective of most organized movements was to spread the gospel of Jesus Christ to millions of Africa's sons and daughters groping in spiritual darkness. To this end, much of the economic strength of the associations and conventions went to the support of an African mission.[23]

These conventions are also political in nature, providing African American Baptists with a venue for power and acknowledgment that is often denied them in the outside world. According to Dr. Benjamin Mays, well-know **theologian**, historian, and the sixth president (1940–1967) of Morehouse College,

> The great importance attached to the political maneuvering at a National Baptist Convention . . . can be explained in part by the

fact that the Negro is largely cut off from leadership in the body politic. The local churches, associations, conventions and conferences become the Negro's Democratic and Republican conventions, his Legislature, his Senate and House of Representatives.[24]

There are reported to be approximately thirteen million African American Baptists, the majority of whom are affiliated with three conventions. These conventions are the National Baptist Convention USA, Inc., the National Baptist Convention of America, and the Progressive National Baptist Convention. The NBCA and the PNBC broke away from NBC, the largest and oldest of the black Baptist conventions. It is important to note that African American Baptists are often dually aligned in their convention memberships. For example, many African American Baptists also affiliate with non-black Baptist groups, such as American Baptist Churches in the USA, the group previously known as the Northern Baptists, who supported the abolition of slavery. Appendix 1 provides details about African American Baptist convention history, beliefs, and challenges.

Conventions are attended by ministers, lay leaders of the church, and members of local congregations. The committee structure of the conventions allows groups interested in similar issues to make policy and to plan programs that can then be enacted by local congregations if they choose. Conventions are also very social events and give life to the familiar statement that "there ain't no party like a Holy Ghost party, 'cause a Holy Ghost party don't stop!"

WHAT CURRENT CHALLENGES FACE
AFRICAN AMERICAN BAPTISTS?
There are a number of issues that face today's African American church, presenting challenges to its survival and creating opportunities to bring new souls to Christ. Among these issues are:
• *The maintenance of outreach strategies.* We need to actively maintain outreach ministries so that we can address the needs of the least, the last, and the lost in our communities. It is essential that the black church understand its role as an institution at whose center is Christ

and whose mission has been and must continue to be compassionate and caring service to others. That service is theological—we must provide to those within our walls the Word of God, a Word that is rich and relevant in the lives of African Americans. Paraphrased, that Word says, "when I was hungry, homeless, sick, downtrodden, distressed, and without, you provided for me." The black church lives its theology through service. Caring and compassionate service is also part of our evangelical mission.

• *Evaluation and accountability*. Although the black church cannot easily assess the success of the church's mission because the objectives that are part of the church's ministry are seldom evaluated by way of measurable standards, striving for evaluation and accountability is still a critical goal. Without vision, the people perish. Without accountability, the church cannot survive. For this reason, Rev. William Shaw, the president of the National Baptist Convention, USA, Inc., restructured the convention around the VISA plan: Vision, Integrity, Structure, and Accountability. Individual Baptist churches must also implement programs of accountability. For example, finances should be transparent; annual reports must reflect line items for every expenditure of the church, including all salaries.[25]

• *The quality of black church leadership*. A hotly debated subject on Tavis Smiley's 2003 "State of the Black Church: Relevant, Repressive or Reborn" was the quality of black church leadership. Discussions focused on the fact that as many as 90 percent of black ministers are not seminary trained. According to Rev. Dr. Jeremiah A. Wright Jr. of Chicago's Trinity United Church of Christ, "You can't be a doctor without going to medical school. And you can't be a lawyer without going to law school," but you can become a minister and hold sway in a pulpit with no training. While no one disputes that God calls ministers to service, those called owe it to God and the people to be well prepared. Our black forebears lost their lives in pursuit of equal educational opportunities for our people. As leaders, ministers must set the example for educational excellence.

For additional information on challenges facing the African American church, see Chapter 7, pages 82–84, for challenges to black church leadership and Chapter 9 for a discussion on the role of African American Baptist churches in response to social issues and needs.

FYI

Based on Lamentations 3:22-23, the following contemporary song provides strong support for the ways in which African Americans exercise their religious faith. Believing in a just God, a God who has been merciful to us in the worst of times, we know that each morning brings opportunities for a new life in Christ.

"New Morning, New Mercies"[26]
It's not for anything I've done,
The mercy God shown through his Son.
I'm blessed beyond what I should be,
The more I stop and think,
It's so hard to believe.

New morning, new mercies,
They are new every day of my life.
Unmerited favor, showered on me from above,
New mornings, new mercies.
. . . Every time I wake up in the morning,
See the dawning; yeah! that's new mercy!
When I'm down he picks me up,
Running low he fills my cup;
Yeah! that's new mercy.

Morning, new mercies.

THAT'S WHAT I'M TALKING ABOUT . . .
- What are the most influential stories that you have heard from your elders about "old-time religion"?
- What are the most important lessons taught by the slaves' acceptance of Jesus into their new lives and traditional cultural practices?

- In what ways does your church participate in the traditional missionary role of the African American church?
- How does your church address the social challenges that it faces in its community?
- What does the song "New Morning, New Mercies" teach about African American religious belief and practice?

PRAYERFUL CONSIDERATIONS

- What are my prayers for the sacrifices of my ancestors to grant me this opportunity for religious freedom?
- What am I willing to commit to God and my church to keep alive its history and traditions, even in the changing environment of today's church?
- How do I show my thankfulness for God's mercies to me?

REFERENCES

- Fitts, Leroy. *A History of Black Baptists.* Nashville: Broadman, 1985.
- Herskovits, Melville. *American Negro: A Study in Racial Crossing.* Westport, Conn.: Greenwood Publishing Group, 1985.
- Jones, Miles Jerome. *Preaching Papers: The Hampton and Virginia Union Lectures.* Hampton, Va.: Martin Luther King Fellows Press, 1995.
- Lincoln, C. Eric, and Lawrence H. Mamiya. *The Black Church in the African American Experience.* Durham, N.C.: Duke University Press, 1990.
- Massey, Floyd Jr., and Samuel B. McKinney. *Church Administration in the Black Perspective.* Valley Forge, Pa.: Judson Press, 1976. Revised Edition published in 2003.
- McKinney, Wade Hampton. *A Study of the Negro Baptist Groups in the United States.* A thesis submitted to the faculty of the Rochester Theological Seminary, April 1, 1923.
- Mays, Benjamin E., and Joseph W. Nicholson. *The Negro's Church.* New York: Arno Press, 1969.
- www.blackandchristian.com.

NOTES

1. Some Africans came to America not as slaves but as bonded servants, craftsmen, and explorers.

2. Craig S. Keener and Glenn Usry, *Defending Black Faith: Answers to Tough Questions About African American Christianity* (Downers Grove, Ill.: InterVarsity Press, 1997), 14.

3. Letter to author from Drs. Ella and Henry H. Mitchell, April 26, 2002.

4. The sacred objects and figures that are central to the black sacred cosmos will differ depending on the particular African religious tradition. See C. Eric Lincoln and Lawrence H. Mamiya, *The Black Church in the African American Experience* (Durham, N.C.: Duke University Press, 1990), 3.

5. While most African Americans are likely to have ancestors who came from the west coast of Africa, the many groups of the region differed by tribe, language, physical appearance, culture, and behavioral practices.

6. Ibid.

7. The first African American churches were Methodist churches that split from white congregations. Because Baptist churches are autonomous, African Americans were easily able to start their own churches.

8. Interview with Rev. Dr. Samuel B. McKinney, pastor emeritus, Mount Zion Baptist Church, Seattle, Washington, February 14, 2002.

9. Lincoln and Mamiya, 20.

10. Born into slavery, Nat Turner inherited a deep hatred of slavery from his mother and grandmother. Able to read and write, Turner received a vision from God to rise up against slavery. On August 21, 1831, he and seven other slaves killed his master. They were joined by seventy-five more slaves and killed sixty more whites. Three thousand state militiamen ended the uprising, killing one hundred slaves not involved in the fighting. Turner was executed on November 11, 1831.

11. Lincoln and Mamiya, 20–21.

12. Ibid., 21.

13. Miles Jerome Jones, *Preaching Papers: The Hampton and Virginia Union Lectures* (Hampton, Va.: Martin Luther King Fellows Press, 1995), 21.

14. Wade Hampton McKinney, *A Study of the Negro Baptist Groups in the United States*, a thesis submitted to the faculty of the Rochester Theological Seminary, April 1, 1923, 1. It is also important to note that many white Baptists, particularly those who held many slaves, supported slavery, resulting in a split in the Baptist convention. See Appendix 1.

15. Ibid., 21.

16. Jacqueline Trussell, "Making Religion Relevant: What Does It Mean to Be Black and Christian?" www.blackandchristian.com.

17. Quoted in Lincoln and Mamiya, 177.

18. Trussell.

19. Many African American Baptist churches have nurses on duty during serv-

ices in the event that people accidentally hurt themselves in a moment of religious ecstasy.

20. This form of ecstatic speaking, not understood by human ears, is thought to be heard and understood only by God.

21. Lincoln and Mamiya, 243.

22. www.blackandchristian.com.

23. Leroy Fitts, *A History of Black Baptists* (Nashville: Broadman, 1985), 24.

24. Benjamin E. Mays and Joseph W. Nicholson, in Jacqueline Trussell, "The Convention Movement of the Black Baptist Church," www.blackandchristian.com.

25. The author notes that many ministers do not agree with her regarding the publication of their salaries. However, as a deacon and a parishioner, the author thinks it essential that church budgets honestly reflect all expenditures, perquisites (such as benefit packages), and income, all defined clearly through line item budgets. For additional information on church budget procedures, see Floyd Massey Jr. and Samuel B. McKinney's *Church Administration in the Black Perspective*, Revised in 2003.

26. "New Morning, New Mercies," Nolan Williams Jr., NEW-J Publishing/ ASCAP, 2000.

6

Let's Just Praise the Lord

African American Traditions of Preaching and Pastoral Teaching

OVERVIEW

In all forms of art, there are those who are merely proficient and those who demonstrate extraordinary skill. African American preachers have demonstrated genius in the art of preaching. Preaching is an essential component of **worship** among **Protestants** that appeals to our core beliefs as Christians. In addition, something about African American lives and experience allows the creative proclamation of Christ's majesty in a unique and captivating way. The African American style of preaching celebrates the good news that Christ is Lord and that his redemption is available to all who believe in him.

While all cultures have homiletic (stylistic preaching) traditions, what distinguishes African American preachers is their culturally specific interpretation of Scripture, their skillful use of emotional content, their understanding of the flow and timing of sermonic materials, and their energetic engagement of the **congregation** as tools for effectively communicating the gospel. According to Henry H. Mitchell, a Baptist preacher and expert on the structure and purpose of preaching, "effective preaching reflects the minister's open receptivity to those life scenes which are noticeably emotional in flavor but which constitute memorable and important stations along the way most people travel."[1]

Those who study the African American **church** agree that preaching, or the manner in which the sermon is presented, is the focal point of the worship service. A secondary but equally important component of African American worship is singing (see Chapter 8 for a discussion of music as a **ministry**). Many African American preachers have deep, resounding voices that enhance their sermons and their singing. Those who sing beautifully and who present portions of their sermons in the ritualistic, syncopated, and rhythmic manner for which African American preachers are revered are viewed by their parishioners as being great orators. As a result, these pastors tend to have large and active congregations.[2]

This chapter will examine the unique preaching style of the African American Baptist pulpit and the ways that sermons and other pastoral teaching tools connect with congregational needs by asking the following questions:

• What is the role of preaching in the African American church?
• Why is emotion essential to the preaching style of African American pastors?
• In what ways do pastors teach their congregations?

THINKING THROUGH MY CHOICE

WHAT IS THE ROLE OF PREACHING IN THE AFRICAN AMERICAN CHURCH?

Jesus said that "one does not live by bread alone, but by every word that comes from the mouth of God" (Matthew 4:4). The preached word is essential to worship because it is based on God's Word. Preaching in the African American church has several distinct purposes. They are:

• *Exegesis:* Exegesis is the process of explaining and interpreting religious texts. Preaching teaches congregations the historical context of the Bible and its relevance and relationship to current events and issues affecting the African American community.
• *Communication:* Sermons are designed to communicate specific messages about the meaning of a certain passage of Scripture, to

address a social issue, or to underscore a theme, such as women who loved Jesus, the challenges of prophecy, or the seven last words of Christ. Sermons can be presented as lessons, testimony, and explanations that include analogies, character sketches, streams of consciousness, or dialogues. Communication in the African American church is often a two-way interaction between the preacher and those gathered for worship. The preacher interprets God's Word, and congregants respond through encouraging statements ("That's all right!" "Say that!" "You better *preach!*"), applause, or personal moments of praise such as shouting or speaking in spiritual tongues.

• *Exhortation:* Another goal of the sermon is to persuade, or to exhort. Preaching urges us to understand the sacrifice of Christ, to believe his promises to us, and to act according to that knowledge.

• *Celebration:* Preaching is an experiential encounter that connects a community of believers to Christ. According to Frank A. Thomas, who has studied the role of celebration in preaching, "the nature and purpose of African American preaching is to help people experience the assurance of **grace** [the good news] that is the gospel of Jesus Christ. Whenever the assurance of grace of the gospel is received . . . the natural response is one of celebration and to praise God."[3] Celebration in worship also serves as a pastoral teaching tool—congregants "will neither remember nor practice that which they have not celebrated."[4]

• *Invitation:* The ultimate goal of preaching is to bring souls to Christ. Sermons in the African American church conclude by "opening the doors of the church," a symbolic act that invites listeners to "make the biggest decision of [their] lives" and "to give [their] hand to the preacher and [their] heart to Christ."

WHY IS EMOTION ESSENTIAL TO THE PREACHING
STYLE OF AFRICAN AMERICAN PASTORS?

Emotion is a gift from God. It provides a tool that helps us connect to one another through the shared experience of our African American history and our experience as we worship together on any given Sunday morning. We are thankful for, happy about, overwhelmed by, and amazed by God's mercies to us. In the context of preaching, emotion is also evidence that African Americans love God; because of the many challenges we have faced, it is impossible to talk about our love of God and his love for us without expressing emotion.

The emotion of sermons is something that preachers must manage responsibly. As Dr. Henry Mitchell has urged, "Every sermon must make *sense*; it must be manifestly reasonable and generally consistent with an orderly understanding of God's creation and our experience in it."[5] It is possible for preachers to present sermons that are emotionally charged but have limited content.

> Howard Thurman reported that his homiletics teacher in seminary once told the class that they were not required to deliver great sermons each time they stood in the pulpit, but they were expected to wrestle with a great idea each time they stood there. What is the big idea? It is a valid question to raise about preaching. Remember the George Bernard Shaw depiction of preaching being like seltzer water—a big fuss over nothing. The preaching enterprise is in some measure of trouble when the trappings of preaching—eloquence, scholarship, voice control, and so forth—are more in evidence than the 'big idea' being presented and with which the preacher is wrestling.[6]

IN WHAT WAYS DO PASTORS TEACH THEIR CONGREGATIONS?

Preachers are also teachers. In all of their roles as **ministers** of Christ, pastors present a viewpoint and system of belief to those who worship under their leadership. The power of their role requires them to use it responsibly. A pastor is a caretaker and leader (see Chapter 7); ministers are known as Christ's undershepherds because they are charged with the care of their congregants. They love and tend to them as Jesus tends his church. Primary pastoral teaching tools and responsibilities are:

• *Christian example:* Ministers of Christ are expected to lead by Christian example, exhibit exemplary personal behavior, and engage in humane and supportive interactions with other church members. While ministers are human and prone to human failings, their esteemed public role mandates that they hold themselves to a high standard.

• *Church management:* Church management or administration is tied to the pastor's role as undershepherd (Acts 20:28). Pastoral **stewardship** requires expert, honest, and accountable management of the church and its resources.

• *Intercession:* Technically, intercessors are "go-betweens," persons who intercede with God on behalf of another. The primary mechanism for intercession is through prayer. Intercessors guide souls to God.[7] "The most frightening moment in a pastor's life occurs with the realization that there are people counting on him or her to light the pathway to an understanding of God and a transforming relationship with Jesus Christ."[8] In the Baptist tradition, while formal intercession is helpful, it is not strictly necessary as we can speak to God for ourselves.

• *Pastoral counseling:* Pastors, viewed as reliable, trusted, and compassionate servants of God, are called upon to provide healing words and wise counsel to the members of their congregation. Parishioners expect their pastors to help them work through spiritual confusions and assist them on their paths to mature relationships with Christ and with one another.

• *Programs:* Pastors are expected to see the needs of their congregations and communities, and address them by providing relevant services.

• *Sermons:* Sermons are the main form of pastoral teaching and are the form that reaches the largest number of congregants. Preachers must be responsible in the messages they give, prayerfully assuring that their sermons are guided by the Holy Spirit and are not an avenue to work out issues of ego or other human failings.

• *Vision:* When ministers are called by God to serve him, they receive a special commission to do his work on earth (Matthew 4:18; Jeremiah 3:15). Because of their training and the maturity of their relationship with Christ, pastors may receive visions from God regarding the manner in which their ministry should develop.

FYI

Consider a few paragraphs of the following sermon, given by Rev. Dr. H. Beecher Hicks Jr. to the Metropolitan Baptist Church of Washington, D.C. The text demonstrates the ways that the African American experience can be used to teach important lessons. This sermon skillfully uses familiar Scripture, rhythmically engages the ear of the congregation, presents dilemmas about which they have questions, connects meaningfully with their emotions, and challenges them to think differently about the position in which they often find themselves.

Let God Be God (Exodus 6:6-7) [9]

Understand the relationship God has with Israel. God has heard their groanings, and God has remembered his covenant. God hears what you say; God remembers what he said. The purpose of God in Israel's life is to position her in a position she has never been before. He does that because he has heard their groanings and remembers his covenant.

This is what God has heard. He has heard that they are strangers, they are outcasts, and they are pilgrims in a foreign land. They are living their lives in a condition of bondage, a position that God did not design for them. In the midst of their bondage they suffer a great burden. They must work from sun up to sun down. They must work to satisfy someone else and never enjoy the fruits of their labor. Because of their burden and their bondage they have lost any sense of their own self-worth, and therefore they must be given new value. They must be invested with new purpose; they must be redeemed.

Here's the point:

God's purpose for you in creation was not bondage.

God's purpose for you was not to be an exile in a foreign country.

God's purpose for you was not to walk in chains, yokes, and fetters.

God's purpose for you is not to live your life under

the strain of heavy burdens, and God does not intend for you to walk around as though you have no value and no self-worth.

THAT'S WHAT I'M TALKING ABOUT . . .

- How do you organize your mind and spirit to learn from the preached word?
- What are your strategies for using what you learn from sermons in your weekly activities?
- What preaching strategies are employed by your minister?
- What does the sermon "Let God Be God" teach about why the powerful design and construction of African American sermons is essential to communicating to congregants components of our religious belief and practice?
- What does the sermon "Let God Be God" teach us about God's understanding of our African American experience? How is the lesson of God's covenant with us relevant to the understanding of our lives and purpose?

PRAYERFUL CONSIDERATIONS

- How do I enact the lessons from Sunday morning into my weekday life?
- What must I do to live my life as God intended?

REFERENCES

- Hicks, H. Beecher. *Preaching Through a Storm*. Grand Rapids, Mich.: Zondervan, 1987.
- Mitchell, Henry H. *Celebration and Experience in Preaching*. Nashville: Abingdon, 1990.
- Proctor, Samuel D., and Gardner C. Taylor. *We Have This Ministry: The Heart of the Pastor's Vocation*. Valley Forge, Pa.: Judson Press, 1996.
- Smith, Kelly Miller. *Social Crisis Preaching: The Lyman Beecher Lectures, 1983*. Macon, Ga.: Mercer University Press, 1984.
- Thomas, Frank A. *They Like to Never Quit Praisin' God*. Cleveland: United Church Press, 1997.

- Wright, Jeremiah A., Jr. *What Makes You So Strong? Sermons of Joy and Strength.* Valley Forge, Pa.: Judson Press, 1993.

NOTES

1. Henry H. Mitchell, *Celebration and Experience in Preaching* (Nashville: Abingdon, 1990), 26.

2. C. Eric Lincoln and Lawrence H. Mamiya, *The Black Church in the African American Experience* (Durham, N.C.: Duke University Press, 1990), 346.

3. Frank A. Thomas, *They Like to Never Quit Praisin' God* (Cleveland: United Church Press, 1997), 19.

4. Thomas, quoted in Mitchell, 30.

5. Mitchell, 21.

6. Kelly Miller Smith, *Social Crisis Preaching: The Lyman Beecher Lectures, 1983* (Macon, Ga.: Mercer University Press, 1984), 81.

7. Baptist belief is that we can each form our relationship with God. In other Christian traditions, such as Catholicism, the priest serves as an intermediary between God and the believer. As head of the Roman Catholic Church, the **Pope** is chief priest and intercessor.

8. Samuel D. Proctor and Gardner C. Taylor, *We Have This Ministry: The Heart of the Pastor's Vocation* (Valley Forge, Pa.: Judson Press, 1996), 31.

9. Rev. Dr. H. Beecher Hicks Jr., "Let God Be God," sermon to the Metropolitan Baptist Church, Washington, D.C., February 24, 2002, 7:45 A.M. service.

7

Lead Me to Calvary

Leadership in the
African American Church

OVERVIEW

Unlike traditional models of corporate leadership, church leadership always starts with *people*. Leadership in the **church** must follow Jesus' example of meeting people's needs by equipping them with what they require to have meaningful lives. While the verb "equip" has a number of roots, its earliest definition appears to come from a Greek word that means "to make whole." The work of church leaders is to provide through the church the tools to make whole all who enter its doors. The most important tool is love; the most important action is the extension of that love to God's people. Church leadership demands attention to:

• *Practical needs:* Church leaders must do as Christ did and assist those who need food, clothing, and shelter to meet their basic requirements or who require assistance with physical illnesses and disabilities. Historically church **ministries** and home mission societies have provided resources that meet practical congregational and community needs.

• *Emotional needs:* Often people who join the church are wounded in some way. They are physically ill, they are saddened by and struggling with difficult life events, they have been in bad relationships, they are active users of or are in the process of recovery from addictions to alcohol and drugs, or they have experienced or continue to suffer from many forms of emotional, physical, and sexual abuse. Leadership requires attention to these needs through a sensitive acknowledgment that they exist[1] and the provision of Christ-centered counseling and formal and informal forms of emotional support.

• *Spiritual needs:* Church leaders have the awesome responsibility of shepherding souls to Christ. In order to do this effectively, they must be well prepared to answer challenging questions regarding Christian beliefs, Baptist doctrine, and the challenges of faith (Hebrews 11:1).

This chapter will address the following questions that relate to leadership in African American Baptist churches:

• What is the leadership structure of the African American Baptist church?
• What are the qualities of effective church leaders?
• How are female leaders accepted in the African American church?
• What is the organizational culture of the African American church?
• What are some of the strengths and weaknesses of the African American church?
• What are the challenges to leadership in the African American church?
• What is the role of church leaders in the larger community?

THINKING THROUGH MY CHOICE

WHAT IS THE LEADERSHIP STRUCTURE OF THE
AFRICAN AMERICAN BAPTIST CHURCH?

The official leadership structure of the African American Baptist church is usually that prescribed by Baptist beliefs (God, congregation, pastor, officers). However, in Baptist and other **denominations**, African American church leadership tends to come from the pulpit. "The black church demands that the pastor lead. Even if he wanted to lag behind in a humble fashion, the people would push him to the front of the army and crush him with criticism if he did not lead them forward."[2]

While up-front leadership is expected of black pastors, and they are given authority by Baptist **congregations** to act on their behalf (with the assistance of the official board), a process of consensus also occurs in congregational meetings. Parishioners have and expect to use the vote afforded them by full membership in black Baptist churches.

WHAT ARE THE QUALITIES OF EFFECTIVE CHURCH LEADERS?

While church leaders bring to their roles a number of charismatic, spiritual, and administrative abilities, effective church leaders:[3]
- see a need and fill it
- don't serve others for personal gain
- are humble, not expecting recognition or tangible rewards for their service
- serve willingly, eagerly, and joyfully
- persist regardless of the difficulty of their assigned task.

HOW ARE FEMALE LEADERS ACCEPTED IN THE AFRICAN AMERICAN CHURCH?

African American women have an impressive history of leadership in secular and religious arenas. Nonetheless, while many traditional African cultures established complementary male and female social roles, African American women have had to struggle against the sexism of the general society and within black institutions. Women tend to be the majority of the membership of black congregations, but their leadership opportunities are often limited by local church policy and national convention guidelines.[4] Some pastors teach that women are not to be in positions of pastoral leadership (Timothy 2:12), although they may be well accepted as leaders in "effective and efficient parachurch organizations, such as missionary societies and women's mite organizations that were significant in the development and maintenance of the local church."[5] Other African American churches are attentive to the biblical teachings of the prophet Joel, who believed that pastoral leadership is a gender-neutral calling (Joel 2:28). Increasingly, black women are pastoring churches, being ordained as deacons, and serving in nontraditional roles of leadership in the African American church.

WHAT IS THE ORGANIZATIONAL CULTURE
OF THE AFRICAN AMERICAN CHURCH?

While African American organizations have no typical structure, they do have common modes of operating. Commonalities of organizational culture in the African American church include:[6]

• *Cultural ethos:* African American organizations have a cultural identity based on a shared spirituality, history of struggle and resistance, belief in the healing qualities of laughter, and traditions of caring for one another.

• *Loyalty:* "In past times relationships had even more importance because our oppression had taught us that we couldn't count on anybody but ourselves. . . . What others may call cronyism or favoritism is our dependence [on] those we know and can count on. That principle is common among people of color."[7]

• *Perceptions of leadership:* African Americans are essentially relational people; our person-centeredness is evident in our expectations of and ideas about how leadership should present itself in our organizations.

◊ Leadership styles: African Americans tend to depend on the leadership and direction of a single, charismatic leader.[8] While this dependence is a common feature of small organizations, African Americans often maintain it in larger settings where it may no longer be effective.

◊ Touching greatness: African Americans value having a personal connection to leaders. However, the value placed on being close to important, charismatic, and influential persons can result in a focus on who leaders are rather than on what they do. In the context of God's church, great leadership is consistently focused on forwarding the mission of the church as established in the **Great Commission**, on meeting the needs of the community of Christ within the local church, and on creating an exciting, vibrant atmosphere where God's work is done, his word is preached, and his people are well-served.

• *Bureaucratic structure:* Larger African American organizations are often top-heavy; there are lots of chiefs and many who aspire to important and visible roles, largely because there are limited opportunities for such leadership outside of the organization. The risk of this bureaucratic structure can be an overemphasis on rules, regulations, and protocols; a tendency to forget organizational mission; and the development of self-serving processes that do not effectively meet the needs of those they are designed to serve—namely, the congregation.

WHAT ARE SOME OF THE STRENGTHS AND WEAKNESSES OF THE AFRICAN AMERICAN CHURCH?

The primary strength of the African American church, and especially of the African American Baptist church, is its independence. Owned by African Americans, it reflects the history and heritage of its members and serves as a center for religious and community activities.

In the church, the relational nature of African Americans is a significant strength and a potential weakness. In small congregations the pastor and other church leaders know the names and histories of all of their parishioners. Larger churches, particularly megachurches, are necessarily less personal, a new reality that creates a challenge for those with expectations of the traditional person-centered church experience. In those settings, many congregants continue to expect direct access to church leaders that may not always be possible. Deacons and assistant ministers can provide some of the attention and care typically expected directly from the church leaders.[9] Large churches also tend to create smaller units, often based on zip codes, that facilitate the relational expectations of African Americans, providing easier ways for church members to become acquainted with and be supportive of one another.

In their book on black church administration, Floyd Massey and Samuel B. McKinney outline additional strengths and weaknesses of the African American church, strengths that can be used to build success, and issues and concerns that church leaders can address through development of administrative structures designed to meet the mission of the local church.[10] The following chart takes a look at those strengths and weaknesses.

WHAT ARE THE CHALLENGES TO LEADERSHIP IN THE AFRICAN AMERICAN CHURCH?

The challenges of leadership in the African American church are to:
• *Remain relevant:* Baptist church leaders must understand the context in which they work on Christ's behalf. While there is

	BLACK CHURCH STRENGTHS	BLACK CHURCH WEAKNESSES
1	Serves as a station of personal affirmation, which attracts large numbers of persons	Often tends toward anti-intellectualism, which gives low priority to financial support of education
2	Provides a rallying point for development of ideas on religion, politics, and issues affecting immediate welfare	Experiences daily confrontation with needs incommensurate with resources available
3	Provides, because of its often limited personal and financial resources, a springboard for creativity through which those limited resources can be overcome	Lacks, in too many instances, a trained and/or committed leadership
4	Tends to impact greatly on the total community rather than just on its members	Tends to nurture a sense of insecurity that disallows intra- and interdenominational cooperation
5	Reposits the history, customs, traditions, and faith of black people	Tends to rely on an oral rather than a written record of organization and administration
6	Provides an arena for ongoing leadership development	

comfort in doing things as they have always been done, Christ's church will only grow through attention to the changing environment in which it finds itself (see Chapter 9, pages 98–101). Remaining relevant also requires an ongoing process of monitoring and assessment to stay abreast of technological advances that might enhance **ministry** and to learn the challenges facing congregants and the external community.

• *Build on history:* The history of African American Baptists is rich. As the church changes, the lessons that history has taught us should be remembered and respected through Christian education classes, sermons, the singing of the old songs of the black church, and the incorporation of meaningful local cultural traditions into services and programs.

• *Address problems:* Historic church weaknesses, such as anti-intellectualism and the reluctance to incorporate new forms of management and technology, must be aggressively addressed by church leaders committed to the growth of Christ's kingdom.[11]

• *Meet human needs:* This is a primary function of the Christian church: to feed the poor, clothe the hungry, heal the sick, and meet God's people where they are.

• *Remain centered on Christ:* Leaders of the church must follow Jesus, a task that requires submission and obedience to God's will, the practice of humility, and dedication to living a disciplined life. It is impossible for church leaders to effectively witness to others if they demonstrate behavior that is incongruent with their stated beliefs.

WHAT IS THE ROLE OF CHURCH LEADERS IN THE LARGER COMMUNITY?

Baptist churches and their leaders are called to be responsive to community needs. See Chapter 9 for a detailed discussion of the ways in which African American Baptists have addressed social issues that affect the community outside their local churches.

FYI

"A Song of Thanks"[12]

. . . For the pumpkin sweet and the yellow yam,
For the corn and beans and the sugared ham,
For the plum and the peach and the apple red,
For the dear old press where the wine is tread,
For the cock which crows with the breaking dawn,
And the proud old "turk" at the farmer's barn,
For the fish which swim in the babbling brooks,
For the game which hide in the shady nooks,
For the Gulf and the Lakes and Oceans' banks,
Lord God of Hosts, we give Thee thanks!

THAT'S WHAT I'M TALKING ABOUT . . .
- What does leadership look like in your church?
- How can your church build on its strengths and work to repair its weaknesses?
- What are the most important lessons that you have learned from your pastor (from sermons, prayers, Bible classes, management style, or personal interaction)?
- What expectations do you hold of deacons, trustees, ministerial staff, and elected officers of the church? Are they met?
- What is your view of women in the ministry? What are your sources of support for or against female ministers?
- What does the poem "A Song of Thanks" teach about the role of church leaders in communicating to congregants the reasons for our religious belief and practice?

PRAYERFUL CONSIDERATIONS
- In what ways do I provide support to my pastor? What is my prayer for the work that my pastor does on my behalf and for all congregants?
- In what ways do I provide support to church officers?
- What is my prayer for the work that church officers do on my behalf and for all congregants?
- How do I participate in the democratic processes of my Baptist church?

REFERENCES
- Bobo, Sharlynn. Researcher on leadership in African American organizations. Lecture on servant leadership in the African American church. Metropolitan Baptist Church, Washington, D.C., February 6, 2002.
- ———. Interview on the organizational culture of African American churches. Metropolitan Baptist Church, Washington, D.C., February 23, 2002.
- Goodwin, Everett C. *The New Hiscox Guide for Baptist Churches.* Valley Forge, Pa.: Judson Press, 1995.
- Lincoln, C. Eric, and Lawrence H. Mamiya. *The Black Church in*

the African American Experience. Durham, N.C.:Duke University Press, 1990.

• McKenzie, Vashti M. *Not Without a Struggle: Leadership Development for African American Women in Ministry.* Cleveland: United Church Press, 1996.

• McKinney, Lora-Ellen. *View from the Pew.* Valley Forge, PA: Judson Press, 2004.

• Massey, Floyd Jr., and Samuel B. McKinney. *Church Administration in the Black Perspective.* Valley Forge, Pa.: Judson Press, 1976. Revised Edition published in 2003.

• www.blackandchristian.com.

NOTES

1.The pastor clearly leads here. Statements made from the pulpit can greatly affect the comfort that certain groups of people feel as they worship and can direct the way in which parishioners care for one another.

2.Floyd Massey Jr. and Samuel B. McKinney, *Church Administration in the Black Perspective* (Valley Forge, Pa.: Judson Press, 1976),37.

3. Sharlynn Bobo, lecture on servant leadership in the African American church,Metropolitan Baptist Church,Washington, D.C., February 6, 2002.

4. C. Eric Lincoln and Lawrence H. Mamiya, *The Black Church in African American Experience* (Durham, N. C.:Duke University Press,1990),44.

5.Vashti M.McKenzie, *Not Without a Struggle:Leadership Development for African American Women in Ministry* (Cleveland:United Church Press,1996),30.

6. Sharlynn Bobo, researcher on leadership in African American organization; interview on the organizational culture of African American churches, Metropolitan Baptist Church, Washington, D. C., February 23,2002.

7.Ibid.

8.In the African American church this might have resulted from our historical reliance on the unique educational status of the black preacher.

9. Bobo, lecture, February 6, 2002.

10.Floyd Massey Jr. and Samuel B. McKinney, *Church Administration in the Black Perspective* (Valley Forge, Pa.: Judson Press,1976),49.

11. More than anything else, anti-intellectualism represents insecurity on the part of those church leaders who fear that highly educated parishioners are more likely to question pastoral teachings.This author was taught early by her father and firmly believes that God can stand up to all questions.Additionally, God does not want us to forget that African Americans fought for educational opportunity, and we should respect and nurture God's gift of intelligence to us.

12. Edward Smyth Jones,"A Song of Thanks," in *The Book of American Negro Poetry* (New York:Harcourt Brace Jovanovich,1969),149.

8

I'm Gonna Do What the Spirit Says Do

The Role of Music in the African American Baptist Church

OVERVIEW

African American Baptists are exuberant in the ways that we celebrate God through music. Music is an essential part of the African American worship experience and is one of the most important ways that we communicate our dedication to Christ and our excitement about the change he has made in our lives. Tied to our African music traditions, affected by the impact of slavery and later social injustices, and constrained by the rules that governed early Baptist worship, African Americans developed through religious music a way to praise God in our unique style.

This chapter describes African American musical worship traditions and asks the following questions:

• Why is music so important to the African American church?
• What are the roots of African American religious music traditions?
• What musical forms represent African American historical religious musical traditions?

THINKING THROUGH MY CHOICE

WHY IS MUSIC SO IMPORTANT TO THE
AFRICAN AMERICAN CHURCH?

In some ways, religious music can be considered to be the performed Word of God. It is certainly a way to praise God. In the African American **worship** service, music is second only to the sermon, and we make it our own, regardless of who has composed it. Religious music and those who perform it are part of a special **ministry**; through our Christian music, African Americans sing of the love of Jesus, acknowledge our ancestral history of pain and suffering, celebrate our current triumphs over adversity, and praise God for his continued goodness to us.

We also use our music to connect meaningfully with one another. During slavery, slaves from the same tribes or language groups were separated from one another. Religious and other forms of music literally gave slaves a new language and way of relating to each other. According to James Cone,

> black music is unity music. It unites the joy and the sorrow, the love and the hate, the hope and the despair of black people; . . . it shapes and defines black being and creates cultural structures for black expression. Black music is unifying because it . . . affirms that black being is possible only in the communal context.[1]

African Americans thrive on social interactions and are attentive to how those relationships present themselves in the church setting (see Chapter 7). Music in the context of worship creates and supports our sense of being a part of a community of believers who have gathered to honor Christ.

WHAT ARE THE ROOTS OF AFRICAN AMERICAN
RELIGIOUS MUSIC TRADITIONS?

African American religious music traditions are strongly tied to African roots and are demonstrated through:
• *Sacred ceremonies and celebrations:* In the African tradition, music was used as part of sacred ceremonies. African music reflects

community beliefs and prayers to the gods and asks for spiritual support to influence personal actions. **Religion** establishes a code of African ethics to define the community and its actions. In African American Christian worship traditions, sacred music is created and used to connect us as a group to the power of God.

• *Cross-Atlantic spiritual traditions:* In Africa, spirituals were a form of oral history. In America, spirituals carried history, common experiences, and hidden messages,[2] and they fully incorporated Christian praise of God.

• *Breaking the rules:* Early Baptist churches, particularly those of General Baptists,[3] were not allowed to use musical instruments. In Africa, drumming was like a long-distance telephone call that allowed those who lived in distant villages to send messages to one another. African American slaves, ever creative while under the watchful eyes of whites, translated the drumming traditions of Africa into a syncopated form of hand clapping and foot stomping, using these rhythms to keep time with vocal music and to serve as musical instruments.

WHAT MUSICAL FORMS REPRESENT AFRICAN AMERICAN HISTORICAL RELIGIOUS MUSICAL TRADITIONS?

"A study of black singing . . . is in essence a study of how black people 'Africanized' Christianity in America as they sought to find meaning in the turn of events that made them involuntary residents in a strange and hostile land."[4] Typically, music in the African American tradition, whether spontaneous or planned, does not follow a **liturgy** or any other plan of worship prescribed by an oversight body. For example, the worship services of the Roman Catholic Church and Anglican/Episcopalian traditions follow a **liturgy** in which the prayers, songs, and Scripture readings are planned in advance for each Sunday of the year. Instead, in the African American tradition, while music is most often part of a planned order of worship within the local Baptist church (one that simply tells what component of the service— songs, Scripture, sermon—happen when), music in the black church more closely follows the dictates of the Holy Spirit. The main ways that African Americans sing in church include the following:

• *Musical forms:* Music in the African American church is sung by the **congregation** and by the choirs, which practice and present their music as part of their ministry to others. Common forms include:

◊ Congregational singing: Congregational singing is a way to get church members and visitors prepared for all portions of the worship service. It allows congregants to "get [their] hearts and minds right" and creates a shared experience among those participating in the service. Because many songs chosen for congregational singing are the traditional songs of the church, this form of African American singing unifies the congregation by teaching these songs to children and new members and by refreshing the historical musical repertoire of established Baptists.

◊ Choral music: Choirs engage in music **ministry** by serving as the church's worship leaders. As **worship** leaders, church choirs set the tone for praise and establish the mood for portions of the service.[5] Their participation in worship allows them to obey the command of Psalm 100:1-2 (KJV) to "make a joyful noise unto the Lord, all ye lands. . . . Come before his presence with singing."

• *African American adaptations of Western music:* Africans have a history of melding our histoical muscial tradition with those we encounter in new lands. African Americans adapted Western religious music to meet our spiritual needs through the following song forms:

◊ Anthems: the first anthems were choral music written by sixteenth-century European **Protestants**. Not surprisingly, African Americans have reinterpreted anthems in a manner that uses our voices to provide unique interpretations of familiar words and tunes. For example, "Let Mount Zion Rejoice" is an anthem with which most African American Baptists are familiar.

◊ Hymns: Hymns are musical meditations that praise the qualities of God and the benefits of a relationship with him. Psalms, written in the third and fourth centuries, were the earliest hymns. Most of the hymns sung by African Americans are adapted from songs in the Anglican (Church of England) and Methodist (Wesleyan) traditions. "Amazing Grace" is one of the most familiar hymns in the African American musical tradition.

◊ Praise songs: The praise song tradition is as ancient as the psalms. The word *psalm* is translated as "praise song." "Holy, Holy, Holy" is a psalm-based praise song. Many modern praise songs, such as "Let's Just Praise the Lord," come out of the **Pentecostal** tradition. In Baptist churches, praise songs are often sung prior to the start of the official worship service as a way for getting "all hearts and minds" prepared to worship.

• *Original African American religious music contributions:* African Americans have contributed to the American musical canon original forms including:

◊ Spirituals: Also known as sorrow songs because many of them portrayed the pain of slavery,[6] these songs are a staple of the African American church. Spirituals fulfilled religious and secular purposes. Their religious purpose was to sing the story of "how we got over"; their worldly purpose was often to provide instructions for escaping from slavery. For example, the song "Deep River" has the lines "my home is over Jordan, I want to cross over into campground." While the religious interpretation of this song is that the singer wishes to go to heaven, slaves also understood this song to reflect a desire to travel north and cross the Canadian border into freedom.

◊ Meter hymns: Meter hymns demonstrate the creativity of early African American Baptist and Methodist worshipers. Because it was illegal for slaves to learn to read, the **worship** leader, often a literate preacher, "lined out" the hymn verses, creating a call and response for congregational singing. "I love the Lord, he heard my cry" is the first line to a meter hymn sung in many African American Baptist churches.

◊ Gospel music: Gospel music is usually thought to have been started in the 1930s[7] by Thomas A. Dorsey, a preacher's son. Considered scandalous at the time, gospel music blended a number of African American traditions, particularly jazz and the blues, into a new way to praise God. One of the best-known gospel songs, "Precious Lord, Take My Hand," was written by Dorsey.

◊ Hip-hop/contemporary gospel music: Hip-hop and other contemporary gospel music traditions sing about Christ in a youthful, urban way. The newest form of African American religious music, hip-hop gospel, is loved by many young people and, in some cases, confuses their elders. However, this form of gospel music follows its historically gospel roots; it has, like the gospel music of the 1930s, found a way to convert a secular music form into a religious celebration that connects with people and brings them to Christ. With its use of syncopated voices and instrumentation, hip-hop gospel is also true to its African roots. Musicians such as Kirk Franklin ("Something About the Name Jesus") and Nolan Williams ("Praise Him") have created richly textured religious music that excites the hearts of many African American Christians.

FYI

"His Eye Is on the Sparrow"[8]
Why should I feel discouraged,
Why should the shadows come,
Why should my heart be lonely,
And long for heav'n and home;
When Jesus is my portion?
My constant friend is he:
His eye is on the sparrow,
And I know he watches me.

I sing because I'm happy,
I sing because I'm free;
For his eye is on the sparrow,
And I know he watches me.

THAT'S WHAT I'M TALKING ABOUT . . .

- What lessons can be learned from the traditional music of the African American church? In what ways are these songs relevant today?
- Why is it important to maintain traditional and modern forms of religious music in the African American church?
- What does the song "His Eye Is on the Sparrow" teach about the role of music in the African American church? What does

it teach about the ways that music is essential to the religious belief and practice of the individual believer?

PRAYERFUL CONSIDERATIONS

- How does the music I hear in worship minister to my spirit?
- How do I keep the power of that ministry with me outside of the context of worship?
- What is my most comfortable form of praise? How might I move beyond my "praise comfort zone"?

REFERENCES

- *African American Heritage Hymnal*. Chicago: GIA Publications, 2001.
- Lincoln, C. Eric, and Lawrence H. Mamiya. *The Black Church in the African American Experience*. Durham, N.C.: Duke University Press, 1990.
- Mapson, J. Wendell, Jr. *The Ministry of Music in the Black Church*. Valley Forge, Pa: Judson Press, 1984.

NOTES

1. C. Eric Lincoln and Lawrence H. Mamiya, *The Black Church in the African American Experience* (Durham, N.C.: Duke University Press, 1990), 347.
2. Christian slave songs often held hidden meanings and messages that alerted slaves to escape routes or that gave them strength to endure their daily challenges.
3. Baptists of the Arminian tradition and believers in free will, General Baptists represent the theological position of the largest group of practicing Baptists.
4. Lincoln and Mamiya, 348.
5. For example, before a prayer, choirs often sing a traditional spiritual or anthem that invokes the Spirit of God. They may sing a more spirited number as preparation for the sermon.
6. W. E. B. Du Bois said of spirituals, "What are these songs? What do they mean? I know little of music and can say nothing of technical phrase, but I know something of men, and knowing them, I know that these songs are the articulate message of the slave to the world." www.northbysouth.com.
7. There is some evidence that gospel music may have begun as early as 1890. See J. Wendell Mapson Jr., *The Ministry of Music in the Black Church* (Valley Forge, Pa.: Judson Press, 1984).
8. Civilla D. Martin (1860–1948), "His Eye Is on the Sparrow," in *African American Heritage Hymnal* (Chicago: GIA Publications, 2001).

9

Guide My Feet

The Role of African American Baptist Churches in Response to Social Issues and Needs

OVERVIEW

African American Baptists have long had arguments about whether it is best to be at the forefront of providing solutions to social problems[1] or if it is better to avoid them, creating within the **church** a social structure separate and apart from those in the world. Despite this ongoing argument, the evidence of history is that many social revolutions have resulted from the intervention of Baptist **ministers**.

> It was King who inspired ministers of all faiths and ethnic backgrounds to understand that there are times when marching in the streets and protesting injustice in whatever arena are continuous with, not separate from or contradictory to, the pulpit ministry. . . . Martin King was no slain civil rights leader; he was a martyred prophet of God who was killed for doing what prophets do. Social crises are exactly where Christian ministers should be found.[2]

As one old preacher was known to caution young ministers, one must guard against being "so heaven-bound that you are no earthly good."

This chapter addresses the important social challenges of the church by asking the following questions:

- What are the primary schools of thought regarding whether Christians are required to address social and cultural issues?
- What social issues have been addressed by African American Baptist churches throughout their history?
- How have African American churches responded to the needs of their communities for programs of social change and relevance?
- What challenges currently face African American Baptist churches?

THINKING THROUGH MY CHOICE

WHAT ARE THE PRIMARY SCHOOLS OF THOUGHT
REGARDING WHETHER CHRISTIANS ARE REQUIRED
TO ADDRESS SOCIAL AND CULTURAL ISSUES?

- *Argument against social intervention:* The biblical argument against intervention in social problems is usually taken from Paul's statement that we are in the world but not of the world (see Romans 12:2).[3]
- *Argument for social intervention:* The argument for intervention holds that the Christian faith recognizes that we are in the world as an important part of it. Support for this argument includes such considerations as:

◊ Christ's example: If we examine the life of Jesus, it is readily evident that he did his work in the world. Jesus met the needs of people where he found them, on the streets, by the banks of rivers, on their beds of pain, in their emotional despair, and when "their backs were against the wall."[4] One such story is found in John 5:1-11.

◊ Role of prophecy: The role of the prophet is to speak truth to power. "It is the speech of the prophet that must be heard from the pulpit of the free. It must be the declaratory of the will of God: 'Thus saith the Lord'—the affirmation of the moral law, the principles of conduct. It must be the speech of judgment: 'Thou are the man.' It must be the speech heralding the new day: 'The Kingdom of God is at hand'; 'Let justice roll on as a flood of waters, and righteousness like an unfailing stream.'"[5] Moses spoke truth to power when, distressed by the enslavement of his people, he told Pharaoh to let his people go. Martin Luther King Jr., a prophetic Baptist preacher, challenged the United States to treat all of its people as equals.

◊ Religion as a social construction: There are many Christian traditions, and their large numbers reflect the fact that while Christ stands alone as Lord and Savior, religions are designed by human beings as ways to honor God. Each religion is developed within its own social, historical, and cultural context.[6] For example, Baptists, believing in the separation of church and state because of their experience in the Church of England, established themselves in Holland, a country where religions could flourish without government intervention.

WHAT SOCIAL ISSUES HAVE BEEN ADDRESSED BY AFRICAN AMERICAN BAPTIST CHURCHES THROUGHOUT THEIR HISTORY?

Believing that God will supply all of our needs, African American Baptist churches have historically focused on addressing social issues that would result in fair treatment regarding equal job, housing, and educational opportunities and the elimination of poverty (Isaiah 11:6). One of the strengths of the Civil Rights Movement was that it did not focus on the rights of African Americans in a vacuum. Instead, it fought for universal freedoms and taught that living up to our social ideals of fairness and equity improved the lives of all Americans (Micah 4:4).

HOW HAVE AFRICAN AMERICAN CHURCHES RESPONDED TO THE NEEDS OF THEIR COMMUNITIES FOR PROGRAMS OF SOCIAL CHANGE AND RELEVANCE?

African American Baptist churches have responded to social needs of their communities through specific ministries and by involvement in social justice issues using a variety of methods, including politics and public policy. While Baptist churches are autonomous and independent of government, African American slave experiences and more recent inequities make many of the acts of the African American church political in nature. For example, when reading was illegal for blacks, the church found ways to teach its members to read. Today, as economic self-sufficiency seems the best route out of poverty, the church is developing strong communities by establishing institutions that support black ownership of homes and businesses. Of course, many famous African American Baptists have also become prominent political figures. Rev. Jesse Jackson ran for president of the United States in 1984 and 1988; Rev. Floyd Flake of Brooklyn held a seat in the United States Congress. The following examples of attention to social needs reflect a time span from slavery to the present.

• *Slave ministers:* Most African Americans did not accept their status as slaves. Many planned and plotted ways to become free. Because slave **ministers** had the respect of their people and access to a regular gathering place, slave rebellions were often led by enslaved ministers of the gospel.

• *Rev. Dr. Martin Luther King Jr.:*[7] Dr. King is perhaps the best-known African American Baptist social activist. Although he was strongly criticized by many African Americans[8] when he began his quest for civil rights in the mid-1950s, he understood the biblical context and modern necessity of his struggle.

Just as the prophets of the eighth century B.C. left their villages and carried their "thus saith the Lord" far beyond the boundaries of their home towns, and just as the Apostle Paul left his village of Tarsus and carried the gospel of Jesus Christ to the far corners of the Greco-Roman world, so am I compelled to carry the gospel of freedom beyond my own home town. Like Paul, I must constantly respond to the Macedonian call for aid.[9]

• *Rev. Dr. Calvin Butts:* The pastor of the Abyssinian Baptist Church follows in the footsteps of his predecessor, the politically and socially active Adam Clayton Powell Jr. Dr. Butts has led successful efforts against police brutality in the city of New York, boycotted local institutions that engage in racist policies, and illustrated the need for AIDS awareness by taking an HIV test. He has been lauded for his activities to bring attention to the ways that tobacco and alcohol companies encourage African Americans to use their products.

WHAT CHALLENGES CURRENTLY FACE AFRICAN AMERICAN BAPTIST CHURCHES?

Challenges to the African American church occur regarding such issues as:

• *Basic Baptist beliefs:* The democratic ideal of the separation of church and state is a core belief of Baptist faith and has been one of its historic strengths. The will of the **congregation** is another core Baptist belief essential to church functioning. Many Baptist churches of all races are becoming more autocratic and less democratic in their structure. History has taught us that dictatorship is the most efficient form of government—a dictator gets things done with limited interference. However, dictatorships tend to be short-lived and terribly divisive. Democracy is much harder, requiring consensus, but it is ultimately successful because it respects the needs and contributions of its many members.

• *Identity and culture:* Knowing and being proud of our history as African American Baptists is a rich resource for understanding why today's church operates as it does. Our history also reminds us of the source of our strength as a people. While progress requires that we adapt our organizations to meet current expectations and needs, it is important to remember "how we got over" and to teach African American Baptist history to maintain the traditions and beliefs of our faith within a changing modern context.

• *Computer and Internet technology:* Largely due to concerns about cost, African Americans are less likely than whites to use new technologies in our homes or in our churches. It is essential, however, that we find ways to access these resources and to use computer and Internet technology to extend Christ's reach to our **parishioners** and communities. Computer use allows us to provide relevant services to our congregation. For example, church offices can computerize membership lists, track finances and the effectiveness of **ministries,** and produce newsletters and bulletins. Though the initial investment may be costly, effective computer use decreases church expenses over time. The Internet is also a tool for providing and receiving necessary and excellent sources of information. Churches can design websites that identify their beliefs and programs, allow communication with church leaders by e-mail, sell sermons on tape and CD, and facilitate the collection of tithes and offerings through secure, online credit card contributions.

• *Technology for ministry and outreach:* Television has proved to be an effective education tool for the general public. Churches have found inventive ways to use television, radio, and the Internet to communicate with their members and to draw outside interest to their church:

◊ Television: Television evangelists such as Creflo Dollar, T. D. Jakes, and **Bishop** Eddie Long have created home-based congregations and new believers through their broadcast programs.

◊ Closed-circuit television: When crowds overflow the sanctuary, closed-circuit television allows congregants to view and participate in the services in another location.

◊ Radio: Many churches have radio broadcasts of their services. Real-time broadcasts allow such innovations as the scheduling of the service to facilitate home communion for the sick and shut in.

◊ Youth appeal: Recognizing that it has a very youthful congregation, University Park Baptist Church of Charlotte, North Carolina, presents its announcements MTV-style. A reporter, seen sitting in the nerve center of a television station, comes on a projection screen and tells congregants of upcoming events and community needs. This presentation alternates with shots of people, lively music, and pictures that illustrate what is being discussed.

◊ Online sermons: The Mount Zion Baptist Church of Seattle, Washington, is but one church that provides sermons on its website in streaming video.

• *Faith-based initiatives:* A controversial topic, faith-based initiatives are governmental programs that provide funding to churches and other religious institutions to implement or enhance social service programs.[10] In fact, black churches have always provided these programs in their communities and have always been eligible for funding from the government. The concern that has been voiced about more recent faith-based initiatives is that they are specifically designed to erode the belief in separation of church and state —a belief that, for Baptists, is central to our faith.

• *Education:* As the premier African American institution, black churches must support education at all levels. Statements from the pulpit, tutorial programs, and scholarship ministries can reinforce the importance of education and its relationship to financial independence, health and longevity, and access to societal resources.

This commitment to education should extend to support of the historically black colleges. Black colleges, many of which educated well-known Baptist ministers and served as the breeding ground for revolutionary social movements, are losing essential sources of government and other[11] funding. Some social commentators believe that this lack of sustainable funding makes them vulnerable to the short-term receipt of funds that may have negative long-term consequences. Black churches and conventions can greatly assist historically black colleges by being financially supportive of their educational missions.

• *Community health:* African Americans suffer disproportionately from a number of medical problems, including diabetes, obesity, prostate cancer, use of addictive substances (alcohol, tobacco, and illegal drugs), and HIV/AIDS. If our bodies are to be the temples of God (Romans 12:1), then church attention to improving our health is an essential form of **ministry**. It has been noted that because it views HIV/AIDS as a disease caused by what is perceived by many as sinful behavior (drug abuse or homosexuality), the African American church has been particularly lax in giving assistance to church members with AIDS or to the systems of families and friends that provide them with practical and emotional support. In addition to helping parishioners strengthen their temples, there has been a more recent move to remind the African American church that Jesus ministered to the sick and calls upon his church to do the same by developing AIDS-based and other health ministries.

• *Incarcerated men:* A disproportionate number of African American men are incarcerated, leading to what some observers call the feminization of the congregation. Many churches have prison **ministries** to bring incarcerated men to Christ. Additionally, churches are developing **ministries** that support and empower young boys and men as one tool for interrupting the cycle of incarceration.

• *Human sexuality:* Biblical injunctions against homosexuality have caused many African American churches to ignore the problems of people who are members of their congregations and families and have, in many cases, contributed greatly to the life of the church. Regardless of whether homosexuality is viewed as a choice or a genetic predisposition, it is important for Christians to remember that we are all on spiritual journeys and must accept one another in love.

• *Gender equality:* Sexism is a long-term problem in the African American church, a place where leaders typically have been male. Church-based sexism is a direct result of social structures that denied leadership to black men in the world outside the church. However, the African American church has been slow to reduce its sexism as external opportunities have improved.

• *Economic self-sufficiency:* Poverty and poor economic opportunity continue to plague the African American community. Many African American churches address this issue by developing community strategies that provide business support, build mixed-use housing, and create banking structures. For example, since 1989, the Abyssinian Baptist Church of New York has overseen more than seventy-five million dollars in urban renewal projects, including the building of six hundred housing units, the locating of a major grocery chain in Harlem, and the purchasing of historic Harlem buildings.

• *Strengthening Christianity through our suffering:* Historian Arnold Toynbee states that the people who have contributed the most to the world have been its historic sufferers. In his estimation, people of African descent have suffered a tremendous amount throughout recorded history. As African Americans work to create a less painful and more triumphant future, those who are Christian can find biblical support for the role of the suffering servant in providing to the world an example of selfless sacrifice for the greater good (Isaiah 53:1-2).

FYI

"God of Our Weary Years" [12]

God of our weary years,
God of our silent tears,
Thou who hast brought us thus far on the way.

Thou who hast by Thy might,
Led us into the light,
Keep us forever in the path, we pray.

Lest our feet stray from the places, our God, where we met Thee,
Lest our hearts drunk with the wine of the world we forget Thee.
Shadowed beneath Thy hand,
May we forever stand,
True to our God, true to our native land!

THAT'S WHAT I'M TALKING ABOUT . . .

- Should the African American church be involved in addressing social problems that affect its community? Why or why not?
- What do the basic beliefs and tenets of Baptist churches suggest about the role of the church in addressing the social and political needs of its members?
- Are you part of a socially active church? In what ways is your church active regarding issues of concern to the African American community?
- What does the prayer "God of Our Weary Years" teach about the possible impact of slavery and more recent forms of social injustice on the religious belief and practice of African Americans? Does it suggest that we have a responsibility to actively address social issues?

PRAYERFUL CONSIDERATIONS

- What are my concerns about the community in which I live?
- What are my concerns about my faith community?
- Should I work to address those social concerns individually, in social organizations, and/or through my involvement in church ministries?

- If so, how can I work to address those social concerns individually, in social organizations, and/or through my involvement in church ministries?

REFERENCES
- Smith, Kelly Miller. *Social Crisis Preaching: The Lyman Beecher Lectures, 1983.* Macon, Ga.: Mercer University Press, 1984.
- Thurman, Howard. *Jesus and the Disinherited.* Boston: Beacon Press, 1976.
- Washington, James Melvin, ed. *Conversations with God: Two Centuries of Prayers by African Americans.* New York: Harper-Collins, 1994.

NOTES
1. The Progressive National Baptist Convention (PNBC) was formed in part to support the social activism of Martin Luther King Jr.
2. Kelly Miller Smith, *Social Crisis Preaching: The Lyman Beecher Lectures, 1983* (Macon, Ga.: Mercer University Press, 1984), 11.
3. The Old Testament teaches that body and soul are one. Paul introduced into Christianity the Greek idea of duality, the concept of body and soul. Since the body decays but the soul lives, some theologians developed the belief that Christians should dedicate themselves to the welfare of their eternal souls only.
4. "The significance of the religion of Jesus to people who stand with their backs against the wall has always seemed to me to be crucial." Howard Thurman, *Jesus and the Disinherited* (Boston: Beacon Press, 1976), preface.
5. G. Bromiley Oxnam, *Preaching in a Revolutionary Age* (1944, 117), quoted in Smith, 4.
6. Smith, 7.
7. Readers may be interested to know that Dr. King was born Michael King. He and his father, for whom he was named, legally changed their names to Martin Luther King in honor of the Protestant Reformer.
8. Many people in the African American community were slow to support the initial actions of the Civil Rights Movement. Citizens and ministers found fault with King's tactics, believing them to be too confrontational and, in some cases, inappropriate for a minister.
9. Martin Luther King Jr., "Letter from a Birmingham Jail," April 16, 1963.
10. Though President George W. Bush established an office for faith-based initiatives soon after his election in 2000, some form of funding for religious institutions has existed for many years under Democratic and Republican presidents.

11. The United Negro College Fund divides funds raised in its efforts among all listed schools.

12. James Weldon Johnson, "God of Our Weary Years," in *Conversations with God: Two Centuries of Prayers by African Americans*, ed. James Melvin Washington (New York: HarperCollins, 1994), 132. This prayer is also a stanza of the Negro national anthem.

10

Total Praise

Living Our Faith

OVERVIEW

African American Baptists thank God daily for the ways in which we have been able to turn struggles into blessings. Our tears, our songs, our laughter, and our dances cleanse us. The memory of our historic pain strengthens us. Our daily victories bolster our spirits. We are gifted at forgiving faults in ourselves and in others. As a 1970s play proclaimed, "Living Black Ain't Easy, But It Sure Feels Good." And it feels so much better when we live our lives with Christ at the center.

This brief chapter presents no new information. Rather, it is designed to serve as a challenge to readers to consider the following important questions:

• What must we do to live our Baptist faith?
• What does it mean to be African American and Christian?

THINKING THROUGH MY CHOICE

WHAT MUST WE DO TO LIVE OUR BAPTIST FAITH?

Living our faith means understanding that people are most successful when we are true to who we are. This book is not titled in a frivolous manner. *Total Praise! An Orientation to Black Baptist Belief and Worship* is meant to remind us that we are a special group of Baptist believers. As African Americans we bring to our faith the unconscious memory of our African heritage, strategies for the survival of our souls and bodies during slavery, a creative approach to living in impoverished urban centers, a drive to overcome modern injustices, and, through it all, an absolute joy for living.

Many readers will remember the movie *Cool Runnings*, the story of the Jamaican bobsled team that participated in the 1988 Winter Olympics. A tropical country, Jamaica was an unlikely entry into the Alpine sport of bobsledding. People around the world thought that the bobsledders were crazy and could not understand why they would choose to be involved in an expensive and time-consuming Olympic event that they would almost certainly not win.

What their critics did not understand, said one bobsledder, was that they were Jamaican. They were people of African descent who had survived slavery and colonialism in an island country through creativity, steadfastness, a belief in working together, and faith in their capacity to overcome obstacles.

When it was time for their Olympic performance, the Jamaican bobsledders ran down the track, jumped into their bobsled, and took off. The old bobsled, which they had lovingly maintained, broke as they traveled down the chute. The Jamaicans got out of their sled, hoisted it onto their shoulders, and walking, carried it across the finish line. The Jamaican bobsledders did not win the Olympic race, but they won the hearts and respect of the people.

This is the lesson of the life of Jesus. Jesus did not conquer the world with armies, with a vast array of modern equipment, or in a manner always understood by others. However, Christ, through his example, won people's hearts.

Living our Baptist faith means living an example that others can see. Following Christ's example, we must strive to win hearts and minds for him. Doing this requires our strong commitment to personal study, congregational **worship, ministry** to others, and a clear understanding of the beliefs and practices that make our faith unique.

WHAT DOES IT MEAN TO BE
AFRICAN AMERICAN AND CHRISTIAN?

African American Christians are part of a special heritage of belief. God attended to us when we lived on the African continent. God has proved himself to us by bringing us out of slavery as he promised. He has given us the victory of the Civil Rights Movement. He has moved us into new homes in the suburbs, stabilized our urban neighborhoods, and facilitated our moves into the highest realms of the corporate and academic worlds. While we continue to be challenged by racism and poor educational and economic opportunity, we know that these things are the result of human actions. We are clearly able to see improvements in our lives, and we know that God deserves the praise for these positive changes. African American Christians believe God, we trust in his Word, we love Jesus as our Lord and Savior, and, even when we don't understand why, we wait on the Lord, knowing that this type of waiting is not passive. African American Christians know that God's blessings are revealed in his time and that the prayerful process of waiting for God to fulfill his will can only make us stronger (Isaiah 40:30-31).

Most importantly, African American Baptists must not forget our social, political, and church histories. We have truly "come over a way that with tears has been watered."[1] As a consequence, it is part of our Baptist and Christian duties to demonstrate continued concern for the least, the last, and the lost among us. We must do for others as Christ does for us. This is our legacy, and it must be our future.

FYI

"We Must Work"[2]

We must work while it is day,
Spreading the Word of God as we go along the way.
We must be willing to do God's will,
Spreading the Word of God till it reaches throughout the hills.
We must witness to everyone we meet in every song we sing.
We must tell them of a soon-coming King!

THAT'S WHAT I'M TALKING ABOUT . . .

- What is your experience of being an African American Christian? What difficulties has Christ brought you through?
- What does the song "We Must Work" teach about the commitment that African American Baptists have made to Jesus Christ?
- What does the song "We Must Work" teach about the commitment that African American Baptists have made to our community of believers and to those outside the walls of the church?

PRAYERFUL CONSIDERATIONS

- How do I express my beliefs to family and friends?
- How is my African American heritage evident in my praise?
- Am I true to my Baptist beliefs? If not, what is it that is standing in my way?
- What must I do to fully commit myself to living my faith on a daily basis?
- What is my prayer for a fully active faith and a commitment to serve Jesus through my Baptist church?

REFERENCES

*Cosby, Camille O. and Poussaint, Renee (Editors). *A Wealth of Wisdom: Legendary African American Elders Speak.* This collection of stories of 50 elders who are over the age of 70 tells their stories in conjunction with the National Visionary Leadership Project (NVLP). The NVLP produced a videotape (*Faith and Human Rights: Legendary African American Elders Speak*) of vignettes from persons important to the life of the church and civil rights movement. Contact NVLP at 1218 16th St. NW, Washington, DC, 20036, 202.331.2700. NVLP would also like churches to nominate community elders for NVLP and/or maintain their own local archives in an effort to codify our oral traditions. Applications are available at www.visionaryproject.com.

NOTES

1. James Weldon Johnson, "Lift Every Voice and Sing," Negro national anthem, 1900.
2. Keith C. Laws, "We Must Work," *African American Heritage Hymnal* (Chicago: GIA Publications, 2001).

108

Appendix 1

Baptist, African American Baptist, and African American Conventions, Denominations, and Religious Organizations

BAPTIST CONVENTIONS AND ORGANIZATIONS

Because no oversight body governs all Baptist churches, many churches choose to affiliate with associations, conventions, fellowships, and other groups. These groups gather based on their specific religious and cultural beliefs and practices, which range from strict to liberal interpretations of Scripture and original Baptist writings.

Baptists first established associations in the 1800s to support their evangelism. The Philadelphia Baptist Association was formed in 1707, and the Charleston Baptist Association started in 1751. Because of significant differences in views on how to practice the faith, divisions among Baptists began to surface. Primitive Baptists do not evangelize; pro-slavery Baptists organized the Southern Baptist Convention; and several groups of liberal Baptists formed the Northern Baptist Convention. The following listing is not exhaustive, but these groups are representative of the differences in doctrine and practice among Baptists.

Unless otherwise noted, the quotations, dates, and membership statistics in this section are from the official websites of the listed denominations (websites were accessed on February 3, 2003). Statistics were then checked through direct communication with officials from the convention or association.

ORGANIZATION	DESCRIPTION
AMERICAN BAPTIST ASSOCIATION *4605 N. State Line Avenue* *Texarkana, TX 75503* *903-792-2783* *800-264-2482*	Consisting of Missionary Baptist churches (associated with Landmark Baptist churches) for which mission work is their primary purpose, the ABA is "a fellowship of Baptist churches who have elected to associate with each other for the furtherance of the cause of Christ on earth." They "believe that love one for another as Jesus loves the believer manifests our discipleship, proves our love for God and symbolizes our authority as New Testament churches."
AMERICAN BAPTIST CHURCHES USA *P. O. Box 851* *Valley Forge, PA 19482-0851* *1-800-ABC-3USA* *1-800-222-3872*	Considered to be one of the mainline Baptist organizations, this group of local and autonomous churches is theologically liberal. "American Baptist congregations are called by God through Jesus Christ to be communities of faith—empowered by the Holy Spirit to live as witnesses and agents of God's love and justice in the church and in the world; vital in worship; dynamic in proclamation; effective in teaching; loving in fellowship; faithful in stewardship; and compassionate in service."
AMERICAN BAPTIST CONVENTION, USA	Same as American Baptist Churches USA (see above)
BAPTIST GENERAL CONFERENCE *2002 S. Arlington Heights Rd.* *Arlington Heights, IL 60005* *1-800-323-4215*	This Swedish American Baptist group believes that "the Bible is [the] only and sufficient authority for faith and our life as Christ's followers. Those immigrant Swedes gathered in *läsare*, 'Bible reader's' groups, so they could know the truth for themselves. They huddled for prayer and mutual support, striving to live pure and holy lives in a corrupt world."

FOUNDING	MEMBERSHIP	WEBSITE
1924— Texarkana, Texas	• 2,000 ABA churches are listed in the roster but there are no official statistics. Their annual meeting is held in June of each year. Churches send 3 voting messengers to the meeting to conduct essential business for the upcoming year. Each church (even those that do not attend the meeting) completes a "church letter" (enrollment form), data from which is recorded in their yearbook.	www.abaptist.org • Newsletter • Sunday school and Bible study curricula • Personal and daily devotions • E-mail member directory • Conference schedule
1907— as Northern Baptist Convention 1950— as American Baptist Churches 1972— as American Baptist Convention USA	• 1.5 million members • 5,800 congregations • 50 states and Puerto Rico	www.abc-usa.org • Newsletters • Media links • History • Policies and resolutions • ABC regional organizations • Judson Press • Statements on American Baptist commitment to the local church, the Bible, mission, service and Baptist identity • *Lectionary*
1844—by Swedish sea captain Gustavas W. Schroeder 1855—founding of the first Swedish Baptist church in the United States (Waconia Baptist in Minnesota)	• 875 churches • 19 ethnic groups	www.bgcworld.org • History and beliefs • Missions and missionary information • BGC email addresses • Ministries • Publications • Services

ORGANIZATION	DESCRIPTION
BAPTIST WORLD ALLIANCE *405 N. Washington St.* *Falls Church, VA 22046* *703-790-8980*	"The Baptist World Alliance is best described as a fellowship of believers around the world. Because Baptists do not have one central authority they choose to work together in the BWA."
BAPTIST BIBLE FELLOWSHIP INTERNATIONAL *P. O. Box 191* *Springfield, MO 65801* *417-862-5001*	One of several "independent Baptist organizations of pastors and churches [that was] established to defend and propagate the fundamentals of historic Christianity and the distinctives of Baptists. Difficulties from within the [Northern Baptist Convention] brought the BBFI into existence."
CONSERVATIVE BAPTIST ASSOCIATION OF AMERICA *1501 West Mineral Ave. Suite B* *Littleton, CO 80120-5612* *720-283-3030*	CBAmerica, a regional network of churches focused on the **Great Commission**, has "historically been known as a movement of evangelical Baptists with a zealous commitment for evangelism, the word of God, and missionary expansion through church planting both at home and abroad."
COOPERATIVE BAPTIST FELLOWSHIP *P. O. Box 450329* *Atlanta, GA 31145-0329* *770-220-1600*	This group describes itself as "a grassroots movement of free and faithful Baptists" who support one another in their mission to live out the **Great Commission**. They are committed to "doing missions in a world without borders," championing Baptist principles and affirming diversity as a gift from God.
GENERAL ASSOCIATION OF REGULAR BAPTIST CHURCHES *1300 N. Meacham Rd.* *Schaumburg, IL 60173-4806* *847-843-1600* *888-588-1600*	A self-described fundamentalist **sect** related to the **Anabaptists**, "the General Association of Regular Baptist Churches was established . . . as a reaction against liberalism in the Northern Baptist Convention."

FOUNDING	MEMBERSHIP	WEBSITE
1905— London, England	• 201 Baptist unions and fellowships • 43 million members worldwide	www.bwanet.org • World aid • Justice and human rights • Evangelism and education • Men's, women's, and youth resources
1950 (approximate date)	• 3,000+ pastors and churches are listed in the Fellowship Directory. • 800+ BBFI missionaries serve in 95 international locations (1996 data).	www.bbfi.org • Doctrinal statement • World mission • Bible colleges • Mission • Resources • Member churches
1947	• 1,200 churches	www.cbamerica.org • Doctrinal statement • Church locator • Resources • Publications
1991—Atlanta, Georgia	• 1,800 churches	www.cbfonline.org • Theological education • Statistics on religion • E-mail services • Events and speakers • Resources
1932	Not available	www.garbc.org • Beliefs • Resources • Partnering ministries • Organizational structure • Publications and religious items • Online church finder

ORGANIZATION	DESCRIPTION
LANDMARK BAPTISTS (Proverbs 22:28: "Remove not the old landmark")	This theologically conservative denomination, which shares some views with the American Baptist Association, is defined by its belief that the church of the New Testament was Baptist, making the Protestant Reformation unnecessary. Most Landmark Baptists do not believe in the doctrine of **grace**, deny the existence of the universal church, and believe that only those who share their beliefs are truly Baptist.
NATIONAL ASSOCIATION OF FREE WILL BAPTISTS *P. O. Box 5002* *Antioch, TN 37011-5002* *615-731-6812* *877-767-7659*	"The Free Will Baptist denomination is a fellowship of evangelical believers united in extending the witness of Christ and the building of His Church throughout the world. The rise of Free Will Baptists can be traced to the influence of Baptists of Armenian persuasion who settled in the colonies from England."
NORTHERN BAPTIST CONVENTION	Formed by Baptists who were against slavery, the Northern Baptist Convention is now American Baptist Churches USA (see page 110).
PRIMITIVE BAPTISTS	Primitive Baptists reject evangelism and the missionary movement. "Primitive Baptists claim the scriptures as their sole rule of faith and practice, and therefore, are not bound to creeds of faith." They profess to obey the doctrines of the original Baptists who claim to be the New Testament church. The term *primitive* hails from the 1800s, at which time it meant "original" and simple. Also known as Old School Baptists. Primitive Baptist services consist only of praying, preaching, and singing (in compliance with beliefs developed around the time of the Revolutionary War, Primitive Baptists do not believe in Sunday school, organized youth programs, display of pictures of Jesus, or use of musical instruments).

FOUNDING	MEMBERSHIP	WEBSITE
Landmark Baptists split from the Southern Baptist Convention in the late nineteenth century.	Not available Landmark Baptists are also known as • Baptist Brides • Historic Baptists • Missionary Baptists (occasional designation)	www.thewayofpeace.org • Church directory • Doctrinal documents • Songs and psalms • Links to landmark sites
Free Will Baptists have 2 lines of founding: 1727—Southern Line (Palmer movement) in Chowan, North Carolina (formally organized into a General Conference in 1921) 1780—Northern Line (Randall movement) in New Durham, New Hampshire (grew rapidly and merged with Northern Baptists in 1935)	• 2,400 churches in 42 states and 14 foreign countries (Southern line)	www.nafwb.org • Articles of Faith • Church Covenant • Conference information • List of churches
1907	Not available	www.abc–usa.org
1896 appears to be the founding of the American branch of Primitive Baptists. "Primitive Baptists claim primary descent from certain Baptist churches in Wales and in the Midlands of England. The views of these Baptists are summarized in the 1655 Midland Confession of Faith."	Not available	www.pb.org (unofficial website) • Articles of Faith • Black Rock Address of 1832 (distinguishes from other Baptists) • Doctrinal abstract • Frequently-asked questions • Historical literature • Audio sermons and broadcasts • Discussion groups • Church links • Online Bible references • Online web station

ORGANIZATION	DESCRIPTION
REFORMED BAPTISTS *c/o Grace Chapel* *P. O. Box 141592* *Spokane, WA 99214*	Historically part of the English Particular Baptist tradition, the formal, doctrinal basis of most Reformed Baptist churches is the 1689 Baptist Confession of Faith. Reformed Baptists believe in the baptism of believers only and that only believers should be members of local churches.
SEVENTH DAY BAPTIST GENERAL CONFERENCE OF THE U. S. AND CANADA *P. O. Box 1678* *Janesville, WI 53547-1678* *608-752-5055*	This evangelical Baptist **sect** keeps the seventh day (Saturday) as the sabbath and describes itself as "Christ-centered, Bible believing people with traditional family values."
STRICT BAPTISTS (Historical Society) *47 The Willows* *Little Harrowden* *Wellingborough* *Northhamptonshire* *England* *NN9 58BJ*	This group also grew from the English Particular Baptist tradition. "Strict" Baptist refers to the practice of restricting attendance at the **Lord's Supper** to those who have been baptized by immersion on profession of faith or who are members of a church that practices closed **Communion**.
SOUTHERN BAPTIST CONVENTION *901 Commerce Street* *Nashville, TN 37203-3699* *615-244-2355*	The Southern Baptist summary of faith from 2000 reads, "Baptists cherish and defend religious liberty, and deny the right of any secular or religious authority to impose a confession of faith upon a church or body of churches. We honor the principles of soul competency and the priesthood of believers, affirming together both our liberty in Christ and our accountability to each other under the Word of God." Southern Baptists are a conservative group who "share a common bond of basic Biblical beliefs and a commitment to proclaim the Gospel of Jesus Christ to the entire world."
WORLD BAPTIST FELLOWSHIP *P. O. Box 13459* *Arlington, TX 76094-0459* *817-274-7161*	"The World Fundamental Baptist Missionary Fellowship [later the name was shortened to World Baptist Fellowship] was established . . . as a reaction against modernist inroads in the Southern Baptist Convention. A training center, the Bible Baptist Seminary, a missionary organization and a publication, *The Fundamentalist*, were established."

FOUNDING	MEMBERSHIP	WEBSITE
1689	Not available	www.farese.com/rbcd/rbcd.htm • Reformed Baptist church directory
1671— Newport, Rhode Island (American founding)	• 70 congregations in North America Churches in over 20 countries	www.seventhdaybaptist.org • Covenant • Definition of Sabbath • History
Not available	• 3 U.S. churches are listed in *The Gospel Standard* magazine	www.strictbaptisthistory.org.uk/ • History • Application • Links • Literature
1845— Augusta, Georgia This group was originally pro-slavery and made a formal apology for this stance in 1995.	• 15.8 million members • 40,000+ churches in the United States • Sponsor 5,000 home missionaries serving the United States, Canada, Guam, and the Caribbean • Sponsor 4,000+ foreign missionaries in 126 nations of the world • 1,221 local associations • 39 state conventions	www.sbc.net • Faith and Facts • Articles of Faith • Missions • Press clippings • Daily devotions • SBC church locator
1928	Not available	www.wbfi.net

AFRICAN AMERICAN BAPTIST CONVENTIONS, DENOMINATIONS, AND ORGANIZATIONS

Most Christian African Americans are members of the Baptist faith and began to form independent churches as early as 1773. While many belong to some of the conventions and groups listed above, African Americans also historically chose to gather in their own fellowships. As African Americans were not usually accepted within the earliest Baptist organizations and their potential membership within those organizations was the cause of significant disagreement and social disruption in later years (related to whether the Baptist church should support slavery), African American conventions were formed and served several purposes. They provided a safe place to gather as a group, gave solidarity to religious and social movements, and established large networks of support within the faith.

The notation *National* frequently distinguishes organizations as being an African American fellowship, while "American" organiza-

ORGANIZATION	DESCRIPTION
FULL GOSPEL BAPTIST CHURCH FELLOWSHIP *9661 Lake Forest Blvd.* *New Orleans, LA 70127* *504-244-9919*	A network of African American Baptists who believe in the bishopric, this relatively new Baptist church organization takes on expressive elements more typical of Pentecostal faiths, such as holy dancing and speaking in tongues. The Full Gospel movement believes that a new religious structure and expressive focus are necessary to reconnect believers to active relationships with the Holy Spirit.
NATIONAL BAPTIST CONVENTION OF AMERICA, INC. (NBCA) *318-221-2629*	This African American Baptist group—formerly known as NBCA, Unincorporated—was the smaller component of the 1915 split from NBCUSA, Inc. They held the strong view that the publishing board should not be owned by any convention of the Baptist church and should be able to affiliate with any group.

tions are often made up predominantly of Caucasian members. Another example occurs with medical associations: the American Medical Association is the mainline organization, and the National Medical Association is smaller and African American.

According to a recent Gallup Poll that was conducted in conjunction with the Interdenominational Seminary in Atlanta, Georgia (http://www.fact.hartsem.edu), there are three predominantly African American Baptist groups: the National Baptist Convention—USA, Incorporated (NBCUSA), the National Baptist Convention of America (NBCA), and the Progressive National Baptist Convention (PNBC). Together these groups represent more than thirteen million African American Baptists. As will be noted in the following descriptions, many conventions were formed because of conflicts over management or social issues within the original National Baptist Convention.

FOUNDING	MEMBERSHIP	WEBSITE
1990s	Not available	www.fullgospelbaptist.org
		• Sermon exchange • Newsletter • Faith-based chat room • Religion news • Conference information
		www.fullgospel.net
		• Online Bible college • Online Full Gospel Mall • Full Gospel television link
1915—NBCA rejected the disputed charter and kept the name National Baptist Convention of America, Unincorporated.	• 3.5 million members	www.nbcamerica.org
		• History • Ministry objectives • Officers • Events • Press releases

ORGANIZATION	DESCRIPTION
NATIONAL BAPTIST CONVENTION, USA INC. (NBC-USA)	NBC-USA, Inc., the largest of the African American Baptist conventions, was formed immediately after the Civil War.
1700 Baptist World Center Drive Nashville, TN 37207 *615-228-6292*	Three African American conventions merged in 1880 to become NBC. Originally the Baptist Foreign Mission Convention joined with the American Baptist Convention and the National Baptist Educational Convention. The three groups met simultaneously in the same location but had separate constitutions prior to their merger. "The mission of NBC-USA, Inc. is to promote home and foreign missions, encourage and support Christian education, publish and distribute Sunday School and religious literature, and engage in other Christian endeavors that may be required to advance the work of Christ throughout the world."
NATIONAL MISSIONARY BAPTIST CONVENTION OF AMERICA *4269 S. Figueroa Street Los Angeles, CA 90037* *888-760-0007 323-235-8905*	Originally part of NBC-USA, this convention was formed because "a national movement was on for the restoration of the basic theological and biblical concepts, practices and ideals of our National Baptist Convention." Other key reasons were to restore "the original focus and concepts of the National Missionary Baptist Convention of America; . . . a convention in which auxiliaries work without conflicts; . . . a convention that recognizes that the church is a divine institution with a sacred mission on earth, and realizes that the convention is not the church, and recognizes that the power and strength come from the church."
NATIONAL PRIMITIVE BAPTIST CONVENTION	African American Primitive Baptists were emancipated slaves who had attended but were not members of white Primitive Baptist congregations. "Although they have followed much of the doctrine and practice [including foot washing to demonstrate humility] of the white Primitive Baptists, the Black Primitive Baptists have set up a national convention and have established Sunday schools and aid societies, all of which are rejected by the whites." See Primitive Baptists on page 114.

FOUNDING	MEMBERSHIP	WEBSITE
1800—merger, see description on page 120 1915—NBC-USA, Inc. resulted from a split within the National Baptist convention. The split was the result of disagreements over the adoption of a charter to govern the National Baptist churches and a conflict over owner-ship of its publishing house. NBC-USA adopted the charter.	• 8.2 million members • 30,000 churches	www.nationalbaptist.com • History • Beliefs • Conventions • Vision statement • President's statement
1880—Montgomery, Alabama 1988—The group originally formed in 1880 was restored to have "a convention that is controlled by its affiliated churches and members while serving the call of Jesus Christ whose divine sacredness the churches are called to respect."	• 1,000 members attended restoration meeting	www.nmbca.com • History • Sermon of the month • Officers • Events • Press releases
1907— This convention was formed by a number of inde-pendent Primitive Baptist churches fol-lowing the Civil War.	• 250,000 members • Number of churches not available	www.natlprimbaptconv.org • History • Beliefs • Officers • Auxiliaries • Conventions • Upcoming events

ORGANIZATION	DESCRIPTION
PROGRESSIVE NATIONAL BAPTIST CONVENTION, INC. *601 50th Street NE* *Washington, D.C. 20019* *202-396-0558*	This convention describes itself as "an association of Baptist churches throughout the world [that is] committed to the mandate of making disciples for Christ. The convention is founded on the precepts of fellowship, service, progress and peace, and seeks to affirm 'the priesthood of all believers.'"
SOUTHERN BAPTIST CONVENTION *901 Commerce Street* *Nashville, TN 37203-3699* *615-244-2355*	Some African American Baptists have joined this convention as it has become more welcoming to different races and ethnicities. The Southern Baptist Convention is now working to place African Americans in staff, management, and board positions. See p. 116.

FOUNDING	MEMBERSHIP	WEBSITE
A 1961 split in NBC-USA, Inc., led to the formation of the Progressive National Baptist Convention. This convention supported the social actions of Rev. Dr. Martin Luther King at a time when they were considered revolutionary and dangerous.	• 2.5 million members • 1,800 churches	www.pnbc.org • News and announcements • Mission statement • History • Reports from president • Ministry reports • Conference news
1845— Augusta, Georgia In 2000, the SBC vowed to have an "ethnic president within five years." This group was originally pro-slavery and made a formal apology for this stance in 1995.	There is no data on African American membership in the Southern Baptist Convention.	www.sbc.net • Faith and Facts • Articles of Faith • Missions • Press clippings • Daily devotions • SBC church locator

MAJOR AFRICAN AMERICAN DENOMINATIONS

In *The Black Church in the African American Experience*, C. Eric Lincoln and Lawrence H. Mamiya present a comprehensive look at the major religions practiced by African Americans. The history of these religions often includes the belief that God created African Americans as the social equals of whites. Blacks sought to create organizations that supported that belief. The development

ORGANIZATION	DESCRIPTION
AFRICAN METHODIST EPISCOPAL CHURCH (AME) *Church Office of Ecumenical and Urban Affairs* *4519 Admiralty Way* *Marina Del Rey, CA 90292* *310-577-8530* *323-299-4988*	The AME Church is unique among churches in that it was the first that was organized to meet the sociological rather than the theological needs of African Americans. In response to being forced to worship in the balcony of white Methodist churches, the AMEC was founded. The AMEC supports more than one dozen colleges and seminaries.
AFRICAN METHODIST EPISCOPAL ZION CHURCH (AMEZ) *P. O. Box 26770* *Charlotte, NC 28221-2549* *704-599-4630*	A **denomination** dedicated to "the liberation of the human spirit," the AME Zion Church, first known as Freedom Church, "was an outgrowth of the Methodist Episcopal Church, and was necessitated because of discrimination and denial of religious liberty." Sojourner Truth, Frederick Douglass, and Harriet Tubman were all AMEZ members.
CHRISTIAN METHODIST EPISCOPAL CHURCH (CME) *4466 Elvis Presley Blvd.* *Memphis, TN 38116* *901-345-0580*	Organized by 41 ex-slaves as the Colored Methodist Episcopal Church, this church is one of three major African American denominations that grew out of **the Wesleyan tradition**. The CME tradition was a move for independence from the faith of slave masters.

of race-based fellowships provided for blacks social dignity and religious freedom. Most black groups were formed by splits from the white Christian churches that blacks had attended as slaves, but many new churches maintained the basic beliefs and distinctives of the original churches. Those changes were most evident in attention given to the social ills that affected newly freed slaves and through variations in the practice of their faith.

FOUNDING	MEMBERSHIP	WEBSITE
1739—founding of the Methodist Church in England 1784—Methodist Church founded in America in Baltimore, Maryland 1787—AMEC formed by a split from the Methodist Church in Philadelphia, Pennsylvania	• 3.5 million members in the United States, Caribbean, and Africa	www.amecnet.org • History • Church structure • Global outreach • Church events • Publications • Schedules
1796—in New York, after splitting from the Methodist Church	• 1.2 million members in the United States, Caribbean, and Africa	www.amezionchurch.org • History • **Bishops** • General officers • Departments • Links
1870—Jackson, Mississippi	• 800,000 members worldwide • 3,000 churches in the United States, West Africa, Haiti, and Jamaica • Today the church sponsors four colleges and one seminary.	www.c-m-e.org • History and beliefs • Episcopal districts • Online church directory • Event calendar • General boards and departments • Chat room • College of **Bishops** • Publishing house

ORGANIZATION	DESCRIPTION
CHURCH OF GOD IN CHRIST (COGIC) *938 Mason Street* *Memphis, TN 38103* *901-525-4004*	This Holiness or Pentecostal urban church is based exclusively in the United States. The church believes in the primacy of God's Word in people's daily lives: "We hold the Word of God to be the only authority in all matters and assert that no doctrine can be true or essential, if it does not find a place in this Word."
BAPTIST CHURCH	There are three predominantly African American Baptist conventions, the National Baptist Convention of America (NBCA), the National Baptist Convention, USA, Inc. (NBC-USA), and the Progressive National Baptist Association (PNBA). Conventions are located throughout the United States and in several foreign countries.
UNITED METHODIST CHURCH (UMC) *InfoServ* *P. O. Box 320* *Nashville, TN 37202-0320* *800-251-8140*	The theological traditions of the UMC can be traced to the Protestant Reformation and **the Wesleyan tradition**. "The Church has endeavored to become a community in which all persons, regardless of racial or ethnic background, can participate in every level of its connectional life and ministry." Forty-two African American members of the UMC have been elected to the episcopacy since 1968.
PRESBYTERIAN CHURCH (U.S.A.) *100 Witherspoon Street* *Louisville, KY 40202-1396* *800-872-3283*	Practicing religion in the **Calvinist** tradition, "Presbyterians are distinctive in two major ways: they adhere to a pattern of religious thought known as **Reformed theology** and a form of government that stresses the active, representational leadership of both ministers and church members." The Presbyterian Church USA has a special commitment to preserving African American Presbyterian history and to spreading their faith in developing countries.

FOUNDING	MEMBERSHIP	WEBSITE
1897—COGIC began in a gin house that was transformed through mighty preaching and confrontations with the devil into the Church of God 1907—COGIC was reorganized in Los Angeles, California	• 5.5 million members • The COGIC sponsors one African American seminary.	www.cogic.org • History • Beliefs and doctrine • Online church directory • Event calendar • National officers
For information on each convention, see the table located on pages 118–123.	• 13.5 million members	• NBCA—www.nbcamerica.org • NBC-USA—www.nationalbaptist.com • PNBC—www.pnbc.org
1784—founding of the Methodist church with small but stable African American participation 1968—In Dallas, Texas, several factions split from the Methodist church to form the UMC.	• 3,500 African American UMC churches	www.umc.org • History • Church leadership • Church finances • Church library • UMC news • Ways to ignite ministry • Mission and creed
1807—Philadelphia, Pennsylvania	• 2.5 million members • 11,200 congregations • 21,000 ordained ministers • 65,000 African American Presbyterians in the United States, Africa, and southeast Asia	www.pcusa.org • History • Congregations • News and events • U.S. and world missions • Publications • Resources

Appendix 2

Appendix 2 presents literature and website resources on Baptist history and thought, the history of African American Baptists, African American Christian belief and practice, and personal spiritual growth. These resources are designed to give readers more information about the topics raised in *Total Praise!* and to provide additional avenues for independent and group study.

The recommended books are available at most bookstores or through online booksellers like amazon.com, bn.com, and borders.com.

BAPTIST HISTORY AND THOUGHT

BOOKS

Freeman, Curtis W., James Wm. McClendon Jr., and C. Rosalee Velloso da Silva. *Baptist Roots: A Reader in the Theology of a Christian People*. Valley Forge, Pa.: Judson Press, 1999. This volume provides the reader with a comprehensive look at Baptist people, leadership throughout the history of the church, primary beliefs and practices, and Baptists' struggles to worship as they believe.

Goodwin, Everett C. *The New Hiscox Guide for Baptist Churches*. Valley Forge, Pa: Judson Press, 1995. This book is the modern adaptation of an original work written over 135 years ago. *The*

Hiscox Guide contains considerable amounts of information about Baptist church history, the organization of the Baptist church, the expectations for Baptist leaders, typical worship structure, important documents and correspondence in Baptist history, basic beliefs, practices, and rituals, and the rights and privileges of membership in a Baptist church.

McBeth, H. Leon. *The Baptist Heritage: Four Centuries of Baptist Witness.* Baptist Sunday School Board—Baptist Book Stores, 1987. This large volume is an excellent reference that many consider to be a definitive work on the history of the Baptist faith.

WEBSITES

WEB ADDRESS	INFORMATION
www.constitution.org/ bcp/religlib.htm	This site provides information about Roger Williams, the founder of the first Baptist church in the United States.
www.gioffre.com/edbc/ beliefs.htm	This site of the American Baptist Churches USA provides information about basic Baptist beliefs and practices.
www.gty.org/~phil/creeds/ bcof.htm	This site provides a detailed and complete record of the 1689 Baptist Confession of Faith.

BAPTIST ORGANIZATIONS, DENOMINATIONS, AND SECTS

BOOKS

Information on Baptist **denominations**, organizations, and **sects** is also available in the references for Baptist history. In the recent past it has been easy to locate encyclopedias of Christian sects.

Most of these resources are now out of print, but used copies can be located by special request from bookstores or at libraries of seminaries and other religious training sites.

Lincoln, C. Eric, and Lawrence H. Mamiya. *The Black Church in the African American Experience.* Durham, N.C.: Duke University Press, 1990. This book is viewed as an excellent reference and resource on the history and sociology of the African American church. It includes specific information about the history, theology, beliefs, and practices of the seven major religious groupings of African Americans.

WEBSITE

WEB ADDRESS	INFORMATION
www.geocities.com/ Heartland/4857/sects.html	This site provides direct links to many Baptist denominations as well as to those of other faiths.

AFRICAN AMERICAN BAPTIST HISTORY, BELIEF, AND PRACTICE

BOOKS

Fitts, Leroy. *A History of Black Baptists.* Nashville: Broadman, 1985. The author believes that "the tradition of Black Baptists is auspiciously pregnant with wholesome instruction, principles and precepts for lay church leaders, pastors, teachers, and students of Christian culture." Focused on the development of the black Baptist church from its slave traditions, Fitts recounts the cultural, theological, and political history of African American Baptists through the 1970s.

Freedman, Samuel G. *Upon This Rock: The Miracles of a Black Church.* New York: HarperCollins, 1985. This book by a former *New York Times* reporter tells the story of the Saint Paul

Community Baptist Church in Brooklyn, a church that, under the leadership of the Rev. Johnny Ray Youngblood, has created a spiritual and social haven for its parishioners. "It has built affordable housing, created a school, replaced brothels and numbers joints with family stores. . . . Here is a church that has found the divine in the pulpit and the streets, that has tempered and tested its spirituality in activism" (front cover blurb).

Massey, Floyd, Jr., and Samuel B. McKinney. *Church Administration in the Black Perspective.* Valley Forge, Pa.: Judson Press, 1976. Revised Edition published in 2003. This book has been updated to provide current guidelines for church administration. The text also explores how the African heritage and slave experience have molded traditions that are significant in black church life today.

Mitchell, Henry H. *Celebration and Experience in Preaching.* Nashville: Abingdon, 1990. African American preaching brings souls to Christ by creating a celebratory atmosphere in which the presence of God is vibrant and evident. This book discusses the strategies for celebrating Christ through sermons.

Thomas, Frank A. *They Like to Never Quit Praisin' God.* Cleveland: United Church Press, 1997. This book discusses the theology, dynamics, and oratory skills that contribute to good preaching.

WEBSITES—See Appendix 1 for website addresses of the major Baptist conventions and organizations.

AFRICAN AMERICAN CHRISTIAN BELIEF AND PRACTICE
BOOKS
African American Heritage Hymnal. Chicago: GIA Publications, 2001. This volume contains congregational music that reflects the historic traditions and newer musical forms of the African American church, particularly the gospel music that is now recognized as an "authentic American art form." In addition, the

hymnal is unique in its presentation of an African American **liturgical year**. The introduction to the hymnal states that it "is probably the most important addition to Protestant hymnody within the past century. . . . The majority Protestant community in the United States has not paid very much serious attention to the exercise of faith and practice in African American life." This volume recognizes the growing impact of many African American musical traditions within our common American culture and in the lives of Christians of many backgrounds.

Lincoln, C. Eric, and Lawrence H. Mamiya. *The Black Church in the African American Experience.* Durham, N.C.: Duke University Press, 1990. This book is viewed as an excellent reference and resource on the history and sociology of the African American church.

McKenzie, Vashti M. *Not Without a Struggle: Leadership Development for African American Women in Ministry.* Cleveland: United Church Press, 1996. The first female AME **bishop** writes about historical and current challenges to female leadership in the African American Christian church.

Murphy, Larry, ed. *Down by the Riverside: Readings in African American Religion (Religion, Race, and Ethnicity).* New York University Press, 2000. With contributions from some of America's most respected African American theologians, philosophers, and thinkers, this book provides a broad overview of African American theologies and practices, focusing on Protestant Christianity, Catholicism, Islam, and many other religions.

Sernett, Milton C., ed. *African American Religious History: A Documentary Witness.* The C. Eric Lincoln Series on the Black Experience. Durham, N.C.: Duke University Press, 2000. "This widely heralded collection of remarkable documents presents a view of African American religious history from Africa and early America through Reconstruction to the rise of black nationalism, civil rights, and black theology of today. The documents—many of them rare, out-of-print, or difficult to find—include personal narratives, sermons, letters, protest pamphlets, early denominational histories, journalistic accounts, and theological statements" (back cover blurb).

Washington, James Melvin. *Conversations with God: Two Centuries of Prayers by African Americans.* New York: HarperCollins, 1994. Prayers are important to the lives of African American Christians. This book, described as a "radiant anthology," presents the prayers of a wide variety of African American life from 1760 to the present.

WEBSITES

WEB ADDRESS	INFORMATION
www.blackandchristian.com	This site has articles of relevance to African American Christians and chat rooms in which to discuss them.
www.beliefnet.com www.bibles.net www.crosswalk.com	These sites provide opportunities for online Bible study.

PERSONAL SPIRITUAL GROWTH
BOOKS
Janis, Sharon. *Spirituality for Dummies.* Foster City, Calif.: IDG Books Worldwide, 2000. This book and the accompanying CD discuss religious and secular forms of spiritual practice in a user-friendly manner.

Miller, Calvin. *Empowered Leader—Ten Keys to Servant Leadership.* Nashville: Broadman and Holman, 1997. Using the example of King David's desire to please God through service, this book presents a model of Christian servant leadership.

Who Is My God? An Innovative Guide to Finding Your Spiritual Identity. Woodstock, Vt.: Skylight Paths Publishers, 2000. While religious persons consider themselves spiritual, spirituality is different from religious practice. It is not an organized practice; rather, it encourages an individual exploration of our best and most spiritual selves. The book assumes that spiritual practice may include unlearning some social and family rules and traditions.

WEBSITES

WEB ADDRESS	INFORMATION
www.ccci.org/laws	Four Spiritual Laws. This Christian website presents four spiritual laws believed to govern our relationship with God.
www.beliefnet.com	BeliefNet. This multifaith website includes chat rooms, spiritual discussion topics, articles on spirituality, prayer circles, and a variety of spiritual research aids.

Appendix 3

The New Hampshire Confession
Articles of Faith[1]

I. THE SCRIPTURES

We believe that the Holy Bible was written by men divinely inspired, and is a perfect treasure of heavenly instruction; that it has God for its author, salvation for its end, and truth without any mixture of error for its matter; that it reveals the principles by which God will judge us; and, therefore is, and shall remain to the end of the world, the true center of Christian union, and the supreme standard by which all human conduct, creeds, and opinions should be tried.

II. THE TRUE GOD

We believe the Scriptures teach that there is one, and only one, true and living God, and infinite, intelligent Spirit, whose name is JEHOVAH, the Maker and Supreme Ruler of Heaven and Earth; inexpressibly glorious in holiness, and worthy of all possible honor, confidence and love; that in the unity of the Godhead there are three persons, the Father, the Son and the Holy Ghost; equal in every divine perfection, and executing distinct but harmonious offices in the great work of redemption.

III. THE FALL OF MAN

We believe the Scriptures teach that Man was created in holiness, under the law of his Maker; but by voluntary transgression, fell from that holy and happy state; in consequence of which all mankind are now sinners,

---

1. Everett C. Goodwin. *The New Hiscox Guide for Baptist Churches.* Valley Forge, Pa.: Judson Press, 1995, pages 264–270.

not by constraint but by choice; being by nature utterly void of that holiness required by the law of God, positively inclined to evil; and therefore under just condemnation to eternal ruin, without defense or excuse.

IV. GOD'S PURPOSE OF GRACE

We believe that the Scriptures teach that *election* is the eternal purpose of God, according to which He graciously regenerates, sanctifies and saves; that being perfectly consistent with the free agency of man, it comprehends all the means in connection with the end; that it is a most glorious display of God's sovereign goodness, being infinitely free, holy, wise and unchangeable; that it utterly excludes boasting, and promotes humility, love, prayer, praise, trust in God, and active imitation of His free mercy; that it encourages the use of means in the highest degree; that it may be ascertained by its effects in all who truly believe the Gospel; that it is the foundation of Christian assurance; and that to ascertain it with regard to ourselves demands and deserves the utmost diligence.

V. THE WAY OF SALVATION

We believe the Scriptures teach that the salvation of sinners is wholly of grace; through the mediatorial offices of the Son of God; who according to the will of the Father, assumed our nature, yet without sin; honored by the divine law of His personal obedience, and by His death made a full atonement for our sins, having risen from the dead, He is now enthroned in heaven; and uniting in His wonderful person the tenderest sympathies with divine perfections, He is in every way qualified to be a suitable, a compassionate and an all-sufficient Savior.

VI. OF REGENERATION

We believe the Scriptures teach that *regeneration*, or the new birth, is that change wrought in the soul by the Holy Spirit, by which a new nature and a spiritual life, not before possessed, are imparted, and the person becomes a new creation in Christ Jesus; a holy disposition is given to the mind, the will subdued, the dominion of sin broken, and the affections changed from a love of sin and self, to a love of holiness and God; the change is instantaneous, effected solely by the power of God, in a manner incomprehensible to reason; the evidence of it is found in a changed disposition of mind, the fruits of righteousness, and a newness of life. And without it salvation is impossible.

VII. OF REPENTENCE

We believe the Scriptures teach that *repentance* is a personal act, prompted by the Spirit; and consists in a godly sorrow for sin, as offensive to

God and ruinous to the soul; that it is accompanied with great humiliation in view of one's sin and guilt, together with prayer for pardon; also sincere hatred of sin, and a persistent turning away from, and abandonment of, all that is evil and unholy. Since none are sinless in this life, repentance needs to be often repeated.

VIII. OF FAITH

We believe the Scriptures teach that *faith*, as an evangelical grace wrought by the Spirit, is the medium through which Christ is received by the soul as its sacrifice and Savior. It is an assent of the mind and a consent of the heart, consisting mainly of *belief* and *trust*; the testimony of God is implicitly accepted and believed as true, while Christ is unreservedly trusted for salvation; by it the believer is brought into vital relations with God, freely justified, and lives as seeing Him who is invisible. Faith cannot save, but it reveals Christ to the soul as a willing and sufficient Savior, and commits the heart and life to Him.

IX. OF JUSTIFICATION

We believe the Scriptures teach that the great Gospel blessing which Christ secures to such as believe in Him is *justification*; that justification includes the pardon of sin, and the promise of eternal life on principles of righteousness; that it is bestowed, not in consideration of any works of righteousness which we have done, but solely through faith in the Redeemer's blood; by virtue of which faith His perfect righteousness is freely imputed to us of God; that it brings us into a state of most blessed peace and favor with God, and secures every other blessing needful for time and eternity.

X. OF ADOPTION

We believe the Scriptures teach that *adoption* is a gracious act, by which the Father, for the sake of Christ, accepts believers to the estate and condition of children, by a new and spiritual birth; sending the Spirit of adoption into their hearts, whereby some members of the family of God, and entitled to all the rights, privileges and promises of children; and if children, then heirs, heirs of God, and joint-heirs with Jesus Christ; to the heritage of the saints on earth, and an inheritance reserved in heaven for them.

XI. OF SANCTIFICATION

We believe the Scriptures teach that *sanctification* is the process by which, according to the will of God, we are made partakers of His holiness; that it is a progressive work; that it is begun in regeneration; that it is carried on in the hearts of believers by the presence and power of the Holy Spirit, the Sealer and the Comforter, in the continual use of the appointed means — especially the Word of God, self-examination, self-denial, watchfulness, and prayer; and in the practice of all godly exercises and duties.

XII. THE PERSERVERANCE OF SAINTS
We believe the Scriptures teach that such as are truly regenerate, being born in the Spirit, will not utterly fall away and finally perish, but will endure unto the end; that their persevering attachment to Christ is the grand mark which distinguishes them from superficial professors; that a special Providence watches over their welfare; and they are kept by the power of God through faith unto salvation.

XIII. THE LAW AND THE GOSPEL
We believe the Scriptures teach that the Law of God is the eternal and unchangeable rule of His moral government; that it is holy, just and good; and that the inability which the Scriptures ascribe to fallen men to fulfill its precepts arises entirely from their sinful nature; to deliver them from which, and to restore them through a Mediator to unfeigned obedience to the holy Law, is one great end of the Gospel, and of the Means of Grace connected with the establishment of the visible Church.

XIV. A GOSPEL CHURCH
We believe the Scriptures teach that a visible Church of Christ is a congregation of baptized believers, associated by a covenant of faith and fellowship of the Gospel; observing the ordinances of Christ; governed by His laws; and exercising the gifts, rights, and privileges invested in them by His word; that its only scriptural officers are bishops or pastors, and deacons, whose qualifications, claims, and duties are defined in the Epistles to Timothy and Titus.

XV. CHRISTIAN BAPTISM
We believe the Scriptures teach that Christian Baptism is the immersion in water of a believer in Christ, into the name of the Father, and Son, and Holy Ghost; to show forth, in a solemn and beautiful emblem, our faith in the crucified, buried, and risen Savior, with its effect, in our death to sin and resurrection to a new life; that it is pre-requisite to the privileges of a Church relation, and to the Lord's Supper.

XVI. THE LORD'S SUPPER
We believe the Scriptures teach that the Lord's Supper is a provision of bread and wine, as symbols of Christ's body and blood, partaken of by

members of the Church, in commemoration of the suffering and death of their Lord; showing their faith and participation in the merits of His sacrifice, and their hope of eternal life through His resurrection from the dead; its observance to be preceded by faithful self-examination.

XVII. THE CHRISTIAN SABBATH

We believe the Scriptures teach that the first day of the week is the Lord's Day; and it is to be kept sacred for religious purposes, by abstaining from all secular labor, except works of mercy and necessity, by the devout observance of all the means of grace, both private and public; and the preparation for the rest that remaineth for the people of God.

XVIII. CIVIL GOVERNMENT

We believe the Scriptures teach that civil government is of divine appointment for the interest and good order of human society; and that magistrates are to be prayed for, conscientiously honored and obeyed, except only in things opposed to the will of our Lord Jesus Christ, who is the only Lord of the conscience, and the Prince of the kings on earth. But that civil rulers have no rights of control over, or interference with, religious matters.

XIX. RIGHTEOUS AND WICKED

We believe the Scriptures teach that there is a radical and essential difference between the righteous and the wicked; that such only as through faith are justified in the name of the Lord Jesus, and sanctified by the Spirit of our God, are truly righteous in his esteem; while all such as continue in impenitence and unbelief are, in his sight, wicked and under a curse; and this distinction holds among men both in this life and after death.

XX. THE WORLD TO COME

We believe the Scriptures teach that the end of the world is approaching; that at the last day, Christ will descend from heaven, and raise the dead from the grave for final retribution; that the wicked will be adjudged to endless sorrow, and the righteous to endless joy; and this judgment will fix forever the final state of men in heaven or hell, on principles of righteousness.

Appendix 4

Church Covenant

This standard Baptist church covenant is recited typically on the first Sunday of the month, often occurring alongside the Communion service. The Covenant reflects Baptist doctrine and serves to reconnect believers to their beliefs, and when done in a group it also serves to reconnect the body of believers to one another. This basic text is subject to revision by congregations "as new insights from the Word of God shall indicate ways in which our faith and life may be brought into closer accord with the teachings of the Scriptures."[1]

MINISTER: It being made manifest by God's Word that God is pleased to walk in a way of covenant with his people, he promising to be their God and they promising to be his people:

PEOPLE: We, therefore, desiring to worship and serve Him, and believing it to be our duty to walk together as one body in Christ, do freely and solemnly covenant with God and with one another, and do bind ourselves in the presence of God, to acknowledge God to be our God and us to be his people; to cleave unto the Lord Jesus, the great Head of the Church, as our only King and Lawgiver; and to walk together in brotherly love,

---

1. Floyd Massey and Samuel McKinney. *Church Administration in the Black Perspective, Revised Edition* (Valley Forge, Pa.: Judson Press, 1976, revised 2003).

the Spirit of God assisting us, in all God's ways and ordinances as they have been made known or shall be made known to us from His holy Word; praying that the God of peace, who brought from the dead our Lord Jesus, may prepare and strengthen us for every good work, working in us that which is well pleasing in His sight, through Jesus Christ our Lord, to whom be glory forever and ever. Amen.

Appendix 5

The Apostles' Creed

I believe in God, the Father Almighty,
    the Creator of heaven and earth,
    and in Jesus Christ, his only Son, our Lord:
Who was conceived of the Holy Spirit,
    born of the Virgin Mary,
    suffered under Pontius Pilate,
was crucified, died, and was buried.

He descended into hell.

The third day he rose again from the dead.

He ascended into heaven
    and sits at the right hand of God the Father Almighty,
    when he shall come to judge the living and the dead.

I believe in the Holy Spirit, the holy catholic church,[1]
    the communion of saints,
    the forgiveness of sins,
    the resurrection of the body,
    and life everlasting.
Amen.

---

1. The word *catholic* refers to the universal church of the Lord Jesus Christ.

Appendix 6

Opening Lines of Song Titles Used as Chapter Headings

The songs chosen as some of the chapter headings for this book were selected to represent spirituals, anthems, and modern music found in today's African American Baptist churches. First lines of songs come from *The African American Heritage Hymnal* (Chicago: GIA Publications, 2001).

CHAPTER	SONG TITLE
ONE	How Can You Recognize a Child of God?
THREE	Guide Me, O Thou Great Jehovah
FIVE	I've Been 'Buked (song title) Ain't Gwine Lay My 'Ligion Down (third verse)
SIX	Let's Just Praise the Lord
SEVEN	Lead Me to Calvary
EIGHT	I'm Gonna Do What the Spirit Says Do
NINE	Guide My Feet
TEN	Total Praise

SCRIPTURE VERSE	AUTHOR AND COMPOSER	OPENING LINES
Romans 8:16	Text and tune: Margaret Pleasant Douroux (1941–)	How can you recognize a child of God?
Isaiah 58:11	Text: William Williams (1717–1791) and Peter Williams (1722–1796) Tune: Traditional meter	Guide me, O thou great Jehovah, pilgrim through this barren land . . .
	Negro spiritual	I've been 'buked and I've been scorned . . . I've been talked about sho's you' born.
Psalm 150:6	Text: Gloria Gaither (1942–) and William Gaither Tune: William Gaither (1936–)	Let's just praise the Lord! . . .
Mark 15:22	Text: Jennie E. Hussey (1874–1958) Tune: William J. Kirkpatrick (1838–1921)	King of my life I crown thee now; thine shall the glory be . . .
	Negro spiritual	I'm gonna do what the Spirit says do; if the Spirit says do, I'm gonna do, my Lord . . .
Luke 1:78-79	Negro spiritual	Guide my feet while I run this race . . .
Psalm 121:1	Text and tune: Richard Smallwood (1996)	Lord, I will lift mine eyes to the hills knowing my help is coming from you . . .

Glossary

This glossary contains words that were boldfaced throughout the book. Except where noted, the definitions are supplied by the author. Although they are not exhaustive, these definitions are designed to contribute meaning to the materials provided in *Total Praise!*

Adherent: A supporter or believer of a religion or philosophy.

Anabaptists: A group of Protestant Reformers who believed in the rebaptism of those previously baptized as children. Only mature adults were thought capable of understanding and committing to a relationship with God. Anabaptist means "rebaptism."

Apocrypha: A set of early Christian writings not included in the Protestant Bible.

Apostle: This term most often refers to the twelve apostles selected by Christ to spread God's word throughout the world. It is derived from a Greek word meaning "messenger."

Arminianism: The beliefs of the Protestant theologian Jacobus Arminius, who rejected John Calvin's view of absolute **predestination**.

Baptism: A religious ceremony in which persons are sprinkled with or immersed in water as an act of purification.

Baptist: A believer in the Baptist **distinctives** of the Christian religion.

Bible: The Christian holy book, consisting of Old and New Testaments. The Baptist faith is considered a New Testament faith.

Bishop: The chief priest, ruler, or teacher of a Christian church, most often in the Catholic and Anglican traditions. The Full Gospel movement of the Baptist church has a **bishopric** structure.

Bishopric: The position, rank, or office of **bishop**. The term is sometimes used to define bishops in the collective.

Calvinism: The religious philosophy of John Calvin, a French Protestant Reformer, whose theology focused on the belief that God has determined beforehand all that will happen (**predestination** rather than **free will**), interpretation of the Bible through the intervention of the Holy Spirit, the sovereignty of God, and the inability of individuals to achieve salvation through their works.

Catechism: A book of questions and answers about religion, used to teach faith-related dogma.

Christology: The study of the life, works, and teachings of Jesus.

Church: This term comes from the Greek word *kuriakon*, which means "belonging to the Lord." "Church" has several definitions: a body of Christian worshipers or believers, a religious organization, a building used for worship, or a religious order. The New Testament word for "church" was *ekklesia* (www.encarta.com).

Communion: Also called the **Lord's Supper**, this ritual commemorates Christ's last meal with his disciples before he was crucified. The Communion ceremony consists of prayers, songs, and the sharing of bread and wine or grape juice, representing Christ's body and blood.

Congregation: A group of people who gather for religious celebration.

Consubstantiation: The Christian belief that the body and blood of Christ coexist with the bread and wine used in **Communion** services. Baptists do not believe in consubstantiation; rather, for Baptists the act of Communion is symbolic of Christ's sacrifice for us and provides for us an opportunity to honor his sacrifice through the ritual of the **Lord's Supper** in which we commune together.

Creed: This term comes from the Latin word *credo* ("I believe"). A creed lists the principal articles of faith of churches or groups of believers.

Crucifixion: A form of execution that involved hanging a person on a wooden cross until death resulted. This is the method by which Jesus was executed.

Denomination: A group of religious believers within a faith. Baptists, for example, are one Christian denomination.

Deuterocanonical: Part of a disputed collection of books of religious Scripture, including all or parts of the **Apocrypha** and the Antilegomena (www.encarta.com).

Disciples: In this context, disciples are original followers of Jesus.

Distinctives: Factors that make a particular faith unique and distinctive from other faiths.

Divinity: The qualities associated with being God.

Dogma: A belief or set of beliefs that a religion holds to be true.

Eastern Orthodox Church: One of the three main branches of Christianity, the Eastern Orthodox Church has three branches, two of which (Orthodox and Oriental Orthodox Churches) split from the Roman Catholic Church and the third (Eastern Right Church) which retains its loyalty to the Church of Rome.

Ecumenical: Relating or promoting the unity of all Christian churches.

Elements: The bread and wine used for the **Lord's Supper**.

Evangelical: Typically relating to Protestant church groups that believe in the absolute authority of the Bible and that **salvation** comes from the personal acceptance of Jesus Christ as Lord and Savior.

Free will: The belief that while God knows our hearts and minds, he has given us discernment to make decisions and mistakes. It is his wish that we live according to his will; our Christian journey is our attempt to do so.

Grace: God's love, mercy, and goodwill.

Great Commission: The commission that Jesus gave to his disciples, to go into the world and proclaim that he is Lord and worthy of all our praise (see Matthew 28:19-20).

Immersion: Baptism that submerges the entire body of the believer in water. This is the **Baptist** form of baptism.

Justification: This Christian theological term describes how the relationship between God and an individual sinner is made right or just through belief in God. The word *justify* means "to make just" or "to make right."

Liturgy: The arrangement of all of the components of public worship.

Liturgical year: Books of common prayer found in Catholic and Anglican (Episcopalian) traditions provide listings of prayers, Scripture, sermon topics, and congregational responses to be used for each Sunday of a calendar year. *The African American Heritage Hymnal* provides a liturgical year that is focused on national and Christian holidays, special events in African American history, and an acknowledgment of the importance of family to African Americans (for example, there are litanies for black mothers and for our elders).

Lord's Supper: Christ's last meal was shared with the apostles one day before his death. Passing out bread and wine, Christ identified these elements as symbols of his body and blood and reminders of his sacrifice for humanity. See **Communion**.

Minister: One authorized to perform religious functions in a Christian, usually Protestant, church and who, in this role, assists (ministers to) others.

Ministry: Services provided in God's name, or the profession of someone called of God (pastor, preacher, reverend, priest, etc.).

Monotheism: Belief in one God.

Omnipotence: All-powerful, an attribute of God.

Omnipresence: In all places, an attribute of God.

Omniscience: All-knowing, an attribute of God.

Parishioner: While Catholic and Anglican traditions use this term to refer to people who live in a parish, a religious district of the church, **Protestants** often use the term to mean a member of a church.

Pentecostal: A large group of faiths that believe in celebrating Christ as the apostles did on the day of Pentecost (speaking in tongues). Pentecostals share many Methodist and Baptist beliefs but tend to believe in more literal interpretations of Scripture.

Polity: The form of church government, including leadership, organization, structure, and policy.

Pope: Head of the Roman Catholic Church, the Pope is believed to have received his authority in succession from apostle Peter.

Predestination: The opposite of **free will**, predestination is the religious belief that God determined all of the world's events at the moment of creation.

Protestants: Those known as Protestants today, of which Baptists are but one of many groups, are the descendents of the earlier Protestant reformers. While sharing basic Christian beliefs, Protestant denominations have different faith practices, **tenets**, and dogma that are specific to each denomination.

Providence: Supply all needs, an attribute of God.

Reformed theology: The beliefs of John Calvin, a French Protestant Reformer, include predestination, the idea that believers cannot achieve **salvation** through their works.

Regeneration: The belief that those who believe in Christ will be reborn, or saved, in him.

Religion: A belief in a higher power. The Baptist higher power is a three-part God (the Father, the Son, and the Holy Spirit).

Resurrection: The return from the dead of Jesus Christ, following his crucifixion and burial in a borrowed tomb (Matthew 28:1-10).

Roman Catholic Church: The oldest Christian church and one of the three branches of mainline Christianity.

Sabbath: The day of religious worship. Most Baptists celebrate Sunday as their sabbath.

Salvation: Acceptance of deliverance from sin by God's **grace** and the sacrifice of Jesus.

Second Coming: Christ promised to return to earth and to return to heaven with the righteous believers (Matthew 24:36; 42-44).

Sect: A denomination of a larger religious group. Originally Baptists were a sect of the Anabaptists. Now, as Baptists are the larger group, they can no longer be considered a sect.

Secular: Nonreligious.

Seventh Day Baptists: Baptists who believe in believer's baptism, congregational **polity**, regenerate membership, and a scriptural basis for beliefs and practice. This group holds that the seventh day, Saturday, is the holiest day of the week. They view worship on this day as a sign of obedience to God and not as a condition of salvation.

Stewardship: The process by which we obey our obligations to Christ by managing our money, time, talents, and other resources in a responsible manner.

Tenet: A doctrine, belief, or principle held as true by a religion, party, organization, or person.

Theology: A field of study that attempts to put logical structure and clear content to the beliefs of a religious faith.

Theologian: A scholar who studies and writes about the components of faith.

Tithing: The practice of giving one-tenth of our income to the church, as a response to God's gracious provision for us.

Transubstantiation: The belief of the Catholic Church that during the consecration the bread and wine become the body and blood of Jesus. Baptists do not believe in transubstantiation; rather, for Baptists the act of Communion is symbolic of Christ's sacrifice for us and provides for us an opportunity to honor his sacrifice through the ritual of the **Lord's Supper** in which we commune together.

Trinity: The belief that God is three persons in one, consisting of the Father, Son, and Holy Spirit.

Triune: Consisting of three parts, as in the case of the Christian **Trinity.**

Upper room: The place where Jesus had the Last Supper with his disciples.

Wesleyan tradition: John Wesley, a former Anglican (person of British descent, baptized as an infant into membership in the Church of England), founded the Methodist church in 1739. He also worked with his brother, Charles Wesley, to establish the musical tradition of the church. A Wesley song familiar to African American worshipers is "Father, I Stretch My Hands to Thee."

Worship: Acts of devotion, adoration, and celebration of God.